YO-ATK-648

The Catholic
Theological Union
LIBRARY
Chicago, Ill.

SEMINARY LIBRARY
PASSIONIST FATHERS

THE DIVINITY OF JESUS CHRIST

AN ARGUMENT

The Divinity of Christ

AN ARGUMENT

TRANSLATED FROM
THE FRENCH OF

Mgr. Émile Bougaud

BY

C. L. CURRIE

SEMINARY LIBRARY
PASSIONIST FATHERS

The Catholic
Theological Union
LIBRARY
Chicago, Ill.

WITHDRAWN

NEW YORK
WILLIAM H. YOUNG & COMPANY
TWENTY-SEVEN BARCLAY STREET
1901

Copyright, 1900,
BY
WILLIAM H. YOUNG & CO

All rights reserved.

Nibil obstat.

E. R. DYER, S.S. D.D.,
Censor Deputatus.

Imprimatur.

✠ MICHAEL AUGUSTINE,
Archbishop of New York.

November 9, 1900.

TRANSLATOR'S PREFACE.

THE design of the author in the great work of which the present volume forms but a fragment—a work completed in five volumes—is to exhibit Christianity in a point of view suited to the present time. The Abbé Bougaud does not purpose to write an apology for the Christian Religion, but to state it simply as a fact, to describe its polity, and to unfold its creed. He considers there is more ignorance of truth than antagonism to it ; and that those who outwardly are the most bitter opponents of Christianity, desire in their inmost hearts to find it.

Christianity then requires to be known. It requires to be exhibited to the world under a form which will arrest the attention of the present age. The method employed in its defense by a Pascal or a Bossuet is not suited to our day.

The first volume of "Le Christian-isme et les Temps présents" demon-strates the necessity of a religion. Then comes the question—what relig-ion? More than eighteen centuries have elapsed since a Man lived and died in Jerusalem who has ever since claimed the homage of mankind. Is this Man God? If He is, if He has founded a religion we must accept it. Natural religion will no longer suffice.

Is Jesus Christ God? The whole question resolves itself into this. The answer to the question is to be found in the contemplation of the life and death, of the doctrine and virtues of Jesus Christ : and this forms the subject of the second volume.

A scientific study of the human beauty of the mind, the heart, and the character of Jesus Christ has been re-served for our age ; and has absorbed the attention of Protestants and Cath-olics alike, and formed a theme for the eloquence of unbelievers.

Whilst yet in its very infancy this study has awakened a sort of enthu-siasm for the Person of Jesus Christ, even in men who have not the faith. It will specially commend itself to those who in Cardinal Newman's words "wish to justify with their intellect all that they believe with their heart ; who cannot separate their ideas of religion from its revealed Object :—but who have an aching dissatisfaction within them, that they should be apprehending Him so feebly, when they would fain (as it were) see and touch Him as well as hear. When, then, they have logical grounds presented to them for holding that the recorded picture of our Lord is its own evidence, that it carries with it its own reality and authority, that His '*revelatio*' is '*revelata*,' in the very act of being a '*revelatio*,' it is as if He Himself said to them, as He once said to His disciples, '*It is I, be not afraid :*' and the clouds at once clear off, and the waters subside, and the land is gained for which they are looking out."

The translation embraces only the author's statement of his argument, its premises and its conclusions. This argument is presented to the English reader, in the hope that it will be received as a valuable contribution to the literature on the Divinity of Jesus Christ. It is recommended in a special manner to the Agnostics, inasmuch as it professes to keep strictly within the bounds of human observation and human reason.

PREFATORY WORDS.

———

When Abbé Bougaud wrote the second volume of *Le Christianisme et les temps présents*, from which this little book is an extract, he was about fifty years of age, having been born on May 24, 1824, at Dijon, in Burgundy, the fatherland of S. Bernard, of Bossuet, and Lacordaire. He describes what sentiments filled his soul on his fiftieth birthday, 24th May, 1874, in a prayer at the close of the introduction to his admirable life of B. Margaret Mary Alacoque.

"O Jesus, from my mother's arms to the ardent years of my youth, I never ceased to believe in that infinite love which is the sap, the divine sustenance of Christianity; and now, at the age that brings to man experience of the world, and if he has been faithful, opens to him the splendors of heaven, I

feel that same infinite love shining on
my head with undimmed brilliancy. It
is true to say, I now scarcely believe in
man's love, for I believe much more in
God's love! Help me, then, O Christ,
O Saviour, O Friend, and may these
my last words, if they are to be my last,
bear to the very depths of souls the
knowledge of that love whose charm I
have tasted, but of whose sweetness I
shall never be able to speak."

Of this love, however, he was able
to speak; and, for many years, until
1890, when death removed him from
the episcopal see of Laval, his learned
and exquisite pen produced many a
volume.

To explain the tone both of deep love
and of melancholy so noticeable in this
prayer, we have to turn to the touching dedication of the Life of B. Margaret Mary:

"To the memory of my mother, to
her upon whose knee as a little child I
learned to know, to love, to adore the
Sacred Heart.—Three months before
her death, June 23, 1873, on my return
from Paray le Monial, my mother be-

sought me to resume this biography, previously undertaken at her request, then interrupted, again taken up, and almost finished in the midst of the first anxiety consequent on her illness, and the inconsolable sorrow of her death. To-day I lay it on her tomb as a last tribute of homage to the heart of that incomparable mother to whom I owe all."

Fittingly does he point out in this filial homage, the abiding influence received from his "incomparable mother." For she had truly formed in her son that tenderness of heart which explains his entire life, just as it pervades all his work.

Pectus est quod disertos facit : Eloquence springs from the heart. Above all, Bishop Bougaud was eloquent. The presence of this splendid gift was revealed to him when, twenty-three years of age, just ordained at St. Sulpice, where he had completed his theological studies, and already, in spite of his youth, professor of dogmatic theology in the seminary of Dijon, he heard in that city Lacordaire, then at the zenith

of his glory.   Like the illustrious Dominican, Abbé Bougaud devoted his
talent to the defence of our faith.   He
was "an eloquent apologist."   Even the
biographies which he wrote form a
chapter of apologetics.   They are intended to demonstrate the divinity of
Christianity from its results.

But his great work is the complete and magnificent demonstration
entitled : *Le Christianisme et les temps
présents*.   Nowhere can his whole soul
be felt as in these pages.   They were
preached, as it were, before being
written.   This is why we do not hesi-
tate to apply to this work what has been
said of his oratorical powers :

"His soul overflows with adoration
and with love.   He becomes seized with
a sort of intoxication from the life-
giving sap that flows from the sacred
tree of the cross, and the moving tones
of his voice betray the interior rapture
that possesses him.   He is then irresistible.   Mgr. Bougaud is truly a man
of his times, and in an orator, or a
writer, whose mission is to gain souls,
if this be not the chief quality, it is, at

any rate, the most winning. One is able to exercise an influence on one's age when one is in sympathy with it, speaks its language, understands its passions and its aspirations, correcting the one and directing the other. Now, Mgr. Bougaud has mastered these things. He has not confined himself to the unchanging, eternal depths of the human soul, though he has sounded them too, but has marked that mobile and passion-tossed element that changes from age to age under the influence of events and environment. His ear has been attentive to the voices of his contemporaries and while he speaks to them of their joys, their sorrows and their dreams, they feel that he has heard the sobbing and the cry, and the echo of it is ever ringing in his remembrance. He is in touch with the living soul of his age."

The success of the work was as great as that of the Conferences of Lacordaire. Like Lacordaire, he had his severe critics, perhaps over severe; but all agreed in admiring in him, as in Lacordaire, the accent of love with

which he speaks of our Lord Jesus
Christ. We need not quote the fam-
ous passage in the great Dominican's
Conferences on Jesus Christ : "There
is a man whose tomb is guarded
by love," etc., or the one in the last
Conference on Life : "One day, at a
corner of the street, in , solitary path,
we halt, we listen, and a voice in our
conscience says to us : Behold Jesus
Christ," etc.

One day, Abbé Bougaud brought the
five volumes which form his Apologetics
to Pope Leo XIII., thinking that His
Holiness had hardly heard of them
before.

—"Ah! *figlio mio,*" answered Leo
with a smile, "I have had your work
in my library for a long while, and every
page I have annotated with my own
hand."

A few months ago, the same Pontiff
declared the present year, closing the
century, a year of Jubilee, a Holy Year,
that, all over the world, there may be
aroused new manifestations of faith
and religion with the special intention
" of satisfying publicly for all that has

been recently said and done against
the Divine Majesty of our Lord Jesus
Christ, such as the renewal in these
times of the blasphemy of the Arian
heresy against the Divinity of Jesus
Christ." *

Such a reparation is necessary in our
own country. Those who are well-in-
formed tell us very sad things about the
actual state of the belief of our countrymen.

It is really appalling. " Outside of
the pale of the Catholic Church," says
a recent writer,† " even among the
most orthodox sects, faith in Christ's
Divinity is built upon shifting sands,
and even as we watch, we can see that
gradually the foundations are being
weakened and parted asunder. In a
word, the current of Protestant thought
is setting towards the system of belief
which denies the Divinity of the Son
of Mary, thus destroying that faith on
which were built the spiritual lives of

* Encyclical *Properate*, May 11, 1899.

† Rev. J. McSorley, C.S.P., *American Ecclesias-
tical Review*, October, 1900,—" Protestantism and
the Divinity of Christ."

thousands, and for the saving of which their hearts' blood had been most gladly shed."

We thought it therefore timely to issue a new edition of this book, one of the best in the whole range of our religious literature — and willingly consented to write these prefatory words.

We shall conclude with a touching incident connected with the history of this book.

" Carpeaux, the celebrated sculptor, was dangerously ill. One of his friends procured for him the volume on Jesus Christ. Its perusal changed the heart of the great artist, who had been far more concerned with his profession than with religion or morality. This book brought him back at once to the sentiments of religion which he had entirely neglected since childhood.

When, after having received the last sacraments, the crucifix was presented to him to kiss, he cried, as he embraced it :

—' My poor, dear Lord, how hast Thou been disfigured !   If I had but a little more strength left, I should love to represent Thee as the good Abbé Bougaud has made me to see Thee.' " *

Our Nineteenth Century is in its last moments. It too has busied itself more with art than with religion and morality. Alas! how Christ has been distorted before its sight! May this little book of Bishop Bougaud help it to find its true Christ, the living ideal that all the ages have adored and loved, the true Son of Mary and the true Son of God.

JOSEPH BRUNEAU.

St. Joseph's Seminary, Dunwoodie, N. Y.
Feast of St. Teresa,
October 15, 1900.

* Mgr. Ricard, *l'Université Catholique*, 15 Juillet, 1890.

CONTENTS.

CHAPTER VI.

CHAPTER VII.

CHAPTER VIII.

CHAPTER IX.

CHAPTER X.

THE
DIVINITY OF JESUS CHRIST.

AN ARGUMENT.

INTRODUCTORY.

AMONG the many questions which claim the attention of the human mind, there is none higher, nor upon the solution of which so much depends, as that which concerns the true character of Jesus Christ. What manner of being, then, is this extraordinary man who, rather more than eighteen centuries ago, in an insignificant kingdom, one of an obscure race, at once laid so irresistible a grasp on the world, " who founded for the whole human race the eternal kingdom of a true and perfect religion ; " * " this Being, the purest amongst the strong, and the strongest amongst the pure, who with

---

* Baur, " Le Christianisme et l'Eglise chrétienne."

9

his wounded hand has lifted empires from their hinges, and changed the course of the stream of ages?"* What is He? Is He a God? Is He a man? Does He owe His origin to a happy accident of nature, to a sublime effort of the human race to produce at last a representative worthy of itself? Or, rather, in contemplating the incomparable beauty of His soul, the greatness of His mind, the yet more wonderful greatness of His heart, and the immense results of His extraordinary life, are we not irresistibly led to recognize in Him something more than man? Is there not a visible manifestation of God through the perfect Humanity of Jesus? And just as when we meet gifted natures, we have only to see their countenance, and to listen to their words, and we say: Here is a soul in which greatness, nobleness, goodness, and genius abide; so we have only to see Jesus, and we are compelled to exclaim: Here is a soul in which the Divinity dwells.

* Richter, "De Dieu dans l'histoire et dans la vie."

Such is the question. Formerly, the unique perfection of the Saviour's Humanity was hardly studied. His Humanity was lost sight of in the splendors of His Divinity, as on Mount Thabor.

Now we pursue another method. An attraction growing stronger day by day leads us, O Jesus, to Thy very sweet and very beautiful Humanity. We look upon Thy feet and Thy hands pierced for us, Thy noble brow beaming with sympathy and genius, Thy Heart beating with immense love,—and thus we begin first to suspect, then to catch a glimpse of Thy Divinity, and soon to fall down in adoration.

The former method was perhaps higher ; the latter more winning. The latter is better suited to an age that cares more for facts than for ideas : an age enthusiastically enamored with the method of observation, and more ready, therefore, to accept the proof which goes back from the Humanity of Christ to His Divinity. Is it not the same method, O Jesus ! which Thou didst point out to the troubled soul of one of Thy disciples? "Thomas, put thy hand into the wounds of my feet and of my hands—put it into the wound of my heart, and be no longer unbelieving." *Et noli esse incredulus.** Oh gentle and untranslatable *noli!* Thomas did not resist it. He beheld the man, and he confessed his God. *Vidit hominem, Deum confessus est.* †

We, O Jesus! are entering the same path. Do Thou help us, and grant, that through the contemplation of the human beauty of Thy mind, Thy heart, Thy conscience, Thy whole soul, we may arrive at the full certainty, at the humble and joyful adoration of Thy Divinity.

* S. John, xx. 27. † S. Aug.

CHAPTER I.

General features of the physiognomy of Jesus Christ.—His mind.—His heart.—His influence.

LET us first look at the physiognomy of Jesus. The physiognomy is the manifestation of the soul through the dust of the body. It is the soul coming forth, so to speak, from its retreat, taking possession of the face, and imprinting on it a beauty which has no equal in the order of created things. "What," says Fénelon, "are all the fires of the sun in comparison to the fire in the glance of a man of genius?" He was right, and yet he spoke but of one characteristic of human beauty. It is not genius only that enkindles: the heart too has its fires as glowing, and more melting, which light the countenance yet more quickly. Nor is the will without its fires. From the will comes that bright and manly flame of courage and of strength, which

13

crowns the human brow with the mystery of beauty.

Now, in all these respects the physiognomy of Jesus is incomparable. In Him the human mind reaches the highest manifestation. "I am the Light," said Jesus Christ. This cannot be called in question. He is the pure Light. Around the greatest geniuses gather clouds and mists, the creation of the senses : around Him there are none. Spots are seen on the sun ; there are none in Him. His mind is full of light ; pouring forth its rays in every direction without stint, and with royal munificence. He expands in fruitfulness on all sides, with an absence of effort such as imagination could never picture.

Where, I ask, have you seen a greater loftiness of character than in Jesus Christ ? Who ever proposed to Himself so high an object ? Who ever reached his object by such simple and spiritual means ? What lightning flashes in His conversation, at once gentle and piercing, which give light but do not dazzle, so natural do they seem ! How He rises all at once to the most sublime heights, and carries you with Him! Or, rather, He does not rise: He always dwells on the heights. If He were going up like a man, we should experience as we went with Him that oppression, that blessed weariness of mounting step by step: and, dazzled Himself with that sublime sight, He would communicate to us His emotion. But it is not so. "He is full," says Bossuet, "of the mysteries of God, but we see that these mysteries do not surprise Him. He speaks of them naturally, as one born in such mystery, and in such glory." *

This calmness in such a light, this absence of effort in attaining heights which so few reach, and in always remaining there, have appeared to some the greatest characteristics of this wonderful mind. But I own that I am yet more struck with its depth. Depth is perhaps of a more divine order than height. It is the characteristic of superior minds, but how rare is it! How much haziness, how much uncertainty

* Bossuet, "Hist. Univers.," Part II., ch. xix.

is there not in the forecasts of the greatest geniuses ! How are they falsified
day by day ! And yet it is an enviable
power this, of being able to penetrate
into the hidden windings of events, and
beyond the present, to foresee and
greet the future. Now this glorious
state is the habitual state of Jesus
Christ. Nothing escapes His penetrat-
ing gaze. Who has not remarked in
the Gospel the intuition with which He
discerns the secret thoughts of the
heart, however deceitful may be the
outward appearance? What a surpass-
ing power He has of casting into the
depth of the soul a single word, full of
mystery ; a word, which, misunder-
stood at first, or despised, is only revealed later to envelop him who has
received it in confusion or in light, according to his inward dispositions !
With consummate skill, with a master
knowledge of the heart of man, by a
short conversation He carries forward
His mission, and takes His place as
master, where that of disciple had been
given Him. He sees into the hearts of
His apostles, and at the very moment

when they are multiplying protestations of devotion, gently but distinctly He tells them of their approaching fall.

And this direct, perfect, and divine intuition of souls is not all. He knows the destinies of nations as He knows the secrets of hearts. The future of Jerusalem is as clear to His eyes as the future of Peter or of Judas. The great revolution that was then beginning, the new world which was to be born at the foot of the Cross; the cross which would draw all to itself, the humble apostles who should teach all nations, the nations who should be converted, one fold inclosing all, and one Shepherd governing all;—He sees all this with a direct certainty, with perfect distinctness. And His vast mind, which, overleaping time and space, travels onwards to the last days of the world, in predicting the ruins of Jerusalem gives us the proof that He knows how the human race will end.

And yet there is no effort, no surprise in His prophetic intuition, any more than there was in His sublime elevation. "There is nothing in the knowledge of

2

the future that causes Him disturbance
or astonishment, because His mind embraces all time. The mysteries of the
future which He proclaims are not sudden and unforeseen lights that dazzle
Him, they are familiar objects, of
which He never loses sight, and whose
images are ever present to Him ; and
future centuries are to His all-seeing
gaze as the light of the present day is
to us." *

But if we would form a true idea of
the whole spirit of Jesus Christ, we
must add to this height and depth a
third and crowning intellectual beauty.
Each of His words is fruitful. It sows
for the future. He says, *Blessed are
the poor. Blessed those who mourn.
Blessed the pure in heart. Blessed those
who suffer persecution for justice.*
Marvelous seeds ! Who shall recount
the harvests that have sprung from
them ? From them have sprung all the
apostles, all the virgins, all the
martyrs, all the benefactors of the
human race. He says, " *Render to*

* Massillon, "Sermon sur la Divinité de Jésus-
Christ."

Cæsar that which is Cæsar's ;" and he
lays the basis of the distinction between
the two powers on which modern civilization rests. He says, "*Our Father
who art in heaven,*" and He sows the
seed of universal brotherhood in true
equality. Every word from His lips is
a germ of indefinite progress.

And yet more wonderful is the language which He speaks. Never have
loftier thoughts been expressed in fewer
words ; never have words, heavy and
material in themselves—the despair of
those who write—been so idealized and
transfigured by thought. They are truly
"spirit and life," according to the noble
expression of Jesus Christ Himself. He
uses the fewest words possible ; short,
transparent words, which show the
spirit that animates them. Science has
found a means of reducing the highest
medicinal and life-giving properties of
nature to the smallest possible compass :
Jesus Christ has done the same. In a
few clear and precise words He has laid
down the eternal laws of things, the
fundamental principles of the family
and society, the causes of the decline of

nations and their remedies, and, above
all, the divine laws of the soul. And
under so simple a form that it is at
once milk for infants and wine for the
aged.

Here, then, we have the spirit of
Jesus Christ—not only in His high and
sublime teaching, and in His profound
knowledge of the human heart and of
the future, but also in the instantaneous
and unlimited fruitfulness of His words,
increasing with time, and producing the
renovation of man, of the family, and
of society. Whence has such a genius
arisen? From whom does He proceed?
Previous ages had sought for Him, but
in vain. None like Him had ever appeared.

And now having studied the mind
of Jesus Christ, let us look at His heart.
We shall find there other gifts, other
charms, but the same manifestation of
the Divinity. Or rather, a still more
powerful manifestation, for the heart
is naturally more beautiful than the
mind : it is formed out of a more
heavenly material ; it is a far worthier
vehicle for the Divinity.

Think how the heart of man is constituted. You will be surprised to see how little the heart of Jesus Christ resembles it. We love, no doubt; we give ourselves to each other. This is our glory, the sign that we come from above. But our love is feeble. Is there any whose love has attained the total surrender of self—the thirst for self-sacrifice? Is there any who has not yearned to descend from that Thabor where self is sacrificed for love?

We all bear about that sad wound in the heart of not being able to suffer long, even for those we love the most. There is but one exception—the heart of Jesus Christ. He loves, and He gives all. And because there is no greater act of love than to die for those one loves, from the first moment of His existence to the last He longs for the accomplishment of His sacrifice. "His hour," as He calls it, that which He awaits with impatience, is the hour when on Calvary His sufferings can equal the excess of His love.

And here is another grandeur of the heart of Jesus, corresponding to another weakness in the heart of man. Precisely because we love little, our love embraces only a few. We shut ourselves up in order to love ; we build a little nest where we place the beings most dear to us—a father, a mother, a wife, children, a few chosen friends. Because we have but a little drop of love, we take care of it : we only give it to a few ; and even in giving these few all the affection we possess, we are not sure of giving them enough. How different is the heart of Jesus ! He loves all, and He loves all with the same ardor. The little ones, the great, the poor, the rich, the just, sinners, the forsaken, those abandoned by the world which has He forgotten ? Is there one He has not loved tenderly, ardently ? Have there been any too sinful for the purity of His Heart, or too common for its nobility ? Has one been found either too great for the Humility, or too little for the Sublimity of this Heart ? It would seem even as though this immensity was not enough ; and we discover in His words, and in His prayers, bursts of love with which He embraces all creatures, and generations which are unknown to us.

To such a heart is joined a purity which I dare not call angelic, for it would be saying too little. He lives in the midst of the world, He sits at table with sinners. He sees at His feet every human weakness, and never has I do not say the shadow of a doubt in the virtuous, but the shadow of an insult from the lips of the wicked, been aimed at Him. Everything has been attacked except the purity of this heavenly Being. And as though it were necessary that this heart, so loving and so pure, should possess an unrivaled halo, It has created a multitude of hearts in Its own image—virginal hearts, loving and pure as Itself.

And the perfection of His beauty is this. Instead of presenting Himself to the world with that sadness which made Pascal say so mournfully, "Our greatest infirmity is to be able to do so little for those we love," He appears, on the contrary, with a calm bearing, with the full certainty of healing, consoling, saving, beatifying those He loves. "Come to Me," He cries, "all ye who are weary, and I will refresh you, and you shall find rest for your souls." Happy heart which can pronounce such a word! Alas! we dare not say it to a father, to a friend, to our children, and He has said it to the whole world! "If any one thirst, let him come to me and drink." Thirst for happiness, thirst for consolation, thirst for holiness, thirst for peace—He makes no distinction. His Heart, feeling itself capable of realizing every dream, becomes yet bolder. "Let not your heart be troubled," I bring you peace—peace which the world cannot give, peace which surpasses all understanding. And not only peace but joy. "Your joy shall be full: your sorrow shall be turned into joy." Happy he who can thus speak to those he loves, who can offer them other than impotent desires, or unavailing tears! But what greatness does not such language suppose! And unless we sorrowfully admit that it is but the illusion of a noble and generous nature, we must recognize in it and greet with admiration—a human heart, no doubt, but a heart unlike any other heart, in which we cannot help perceiving an evident manifestation of the Divinity.

Strength is the third attribute of human beauty. We have it here in its highest expression. Jesus Christ has every form of strength : the strength of modesty in His triumph in the midst of the enthusiasm of the multitude : the strength of patience with the self-will of His disciples, the cavils of the Pharisees, and the deceitfulness of the chief priests : the strength of peace and joy in the midst of injuries, buffetings, spittings, scourgings : and what is still more marvelous, the strength of resignation in anguish, when beaten down by the most fearful exhaustion of nature. Such unlimited courage and calm dignity in the midst of circumstances so well calculated to baffle and discourage, challenge the noblest effort of the human will. And yet there is more beyond. He has given a still more wonderful and supreme manifestation of strength in the way in which He has lifted up the world, according to His expression, *"I will draw all things to Myself."*

Archimedes said, "Give me a fulcrum and I will move the world." Jesus Christ has moved the world, and He had no need of a fulcrum. He took twelve poor, rude artisans—men without genius, and without learning,—and He did, what is stranger than to move the world : He changed it, He improved it, He transformed it. And what is more remarkable, He accomplished this change after His death. During His life He did nothing. He died abandoned on a cross. But it was then, as He had predicted,—when He had disappeared from earth, and it seemed as though His work were extinct, and had vanished with Him, it was then that he proved His strength by miracles from beyond the grave, and that from the depth of the sepulchre in which this work was thought to be forever buried, it re-appeared suddenly, full of an endless life, and an eternal fruitfulness.

It seems almost useless to add, in finishing this first outline, that these divine beauties in the physiognomy of Jesus Christ—beauty of mind, beauty of goodness, and of love, of strength, and of courage, are perfectly balanced. You cannot discover either gap, or weakness, or stain, or exaggeration, or effort. Each faculty reaches its highest degree of intensity, but it is impossible to mention one that eclipses the others. They blend harmoniously together, and in Him and in His life we find a tranquil grandeur, a sweet simplicity, and a sublime peace.

From time to time the human race has produced wonderful beings, but none that can be compared with Jesus Christ. He has everything, and in an unlimited measure. In Him, thoughts, words, poetry, eloquence, love, power over men, and immense results, every gift, and every power are united, and in such perfection that the mind which has meditated the life of Jesus Christ can conceive nothing greater.

And this is the meaning of the word "Son of Man" which appears in every page of the Gospel. Jesus Christ is not only a son of man like all the descendants of Adam : He is *the* Son of Man in an absolute sense : the pure, perfect, beautiful ideal man : the fairest flower, the choicest fruit the earth has ever produced, or rather the one fair, perfect flower that has budded forth from the tree of Adam.

CHAPTER II.

Certain special features in the physiognomy of
    Jesus Christ.—General agreement of all
    great minds that this physiognomy points
    to an unique character.

To continue. These are but a few
features, and faintly traced, of the physiognomy of Jesus Christ. According
as criticism becomes more searching,
observation more thoughtful and more
exact, features are discovered in the
character of Christ which the ancient
apologists did not suspect. Christ
stands forth under the gaze of criticism,
like the firmament when examined with
the powerful instruments of modern
science.

Beyond the definite qualities of which
we have just spoken, and which, carried
to their highest perfection and harmoniously blended together, stamp such a
royal human beauty on the physiognomy of Jesus Christ, we begin to dis-

cover in Him what is less easy to lay hold of, what is without limit and bounds. You feel that He is man, but always that He is more than man. There is something of the universal and the inexhaustible which warns you that the ordinary limits of human nature have been passed. Consider, one by one, His moral perfection, His personality, His mind ; you may discover the form, you will never fathom the depth.

The depth of His moral perfection ! You will find it when you can find anything that can be compared to it. But where will you find this ? I will not speak of antiquity : such an ideal was not even imagined. "Jesus by his greatness and goodness," says Channing, " throws all other human attainments into obscurity." * And not only the human perfections of those who preceded, but also of those who followed Him. Such perfections even which owed their origin to Him : for His appearance was like a flash of lightning which revealed an ideal unknown till

* Channing, "The Imitableness of Christ's Character."

then, and which created an all-absorbing desire to imitate Him. For eighteen centuries has this Ideal been before the world, for eighteen centuries millions of men have tried to reproduce it, and proportioned to the closeness of their copy is the beauty to which they attain ;—but to none has it been given to equal it. In these numberless imitations there are many that challenge admiration, some by their purity, some by their strength, but not one that can compare even at a distance with the beauty of Jesus : for the unique beauty of Jesus surpasses not only all created beauty—it is without limit. No ideal prepared the way for it.

You know what happens when we find ourselves face to face with beauty. We contemplate it with delight, and the contemplation gives us wings by which we rise yet higher. We perceive a superior beauty, of which all created beauty, however dazzling it may be, is but the incomplete expression. And however high we rise, however great the effort of the imagination, the ideal still recedes from us,

filling us with despair, provoking our
efforts by its lofty sublimity, and calling into existence the highest art, because genius can never realize the objects of its contemplation. But when
Jesus Christ is in question, all this is
reversed. We do not leave the reality
to run after the ideal ; it is the reality
that we cannot reach. All our efforts
to find an ideal Jesus Christ, that is to
say a beauty distinct from the beauty
which He realizes and superior to it,
are vain. In contemplating Jesus
Christ it is not our ideal that we see ris-
ing, escaping from us : it is He, He
Himself, He as portrayed in the Gospels, who rises, and escapes from us,
whom we cannot reach, either by the
pencil or the chisel, either by the pen
or by the heart. It was this incapacity
of reproducing such beauty, which drew
tears from the blessed Angelico of
Fiesole ; it was this which caused the
brush to fall from the powerful hand of
Leonardo, it was this which caused a
Bossuet and a Pascal to despair. For
the first, perhaps for the only time in
the history of art, its highest perfection

falls short of the truth, and the imagination even of genius fails to idealize the reality.

This reflection alone ought to be sufficient to make every serious mind recognize that the character of Jesus Christ, although truly human and natural, has a superhuman elevation; but I would have you consider something yet more wonderful, a further perfection much more inexplicable. We have found no limit to His moral beauty, to His perfection : let us now seek the limit to His personality. Personality is limited by place, time, and race. However great a man may be, he was born here, he lived there, he sprang from a certain race, he carries the stamp of that race. Look at the greatest men : they belong to their time. They eagerly espouse its interests, passions, joys, and griefs. We observe this in politicians, in lawgivers, in conquerors. On what would they depend to govern the world, and to raise it, if they did not belong to their time ? But do not even mere abstract thinkers, solitary speculators, poets, philosophers,

3

artists, those whose life, consecrated to
the worship of the ideal, goes deeper into human nature and passes less quickly,
do not they also belong to their time?
Through the music of their poems, do
we not hear mingled with the voice of
human nature, the voice of their age:
mingled with the sighs of the human
soul, do we not hear the sighs of the
people, of the century, of the city where
that human soul prayed, wept, suffered,
and loved. Call over the roll of great
men: Homer, Job, Æschylus, Isaiah,
Socrates, Phidias, Sophocles, Plato,
Virgil, Tacitus, Dante, Michael Angelo,
Shakespeare, Milton, Corneille, Racine,
Bossuet. What are they?—the incar-
nations of Greece, of Arabia, of Judea,
of pagan Rome, of Christian Italy, of
Spain, of France, of England. And the
greater they are, the more perfectly
they embody in themselves, with the
genius of the human race, the genius
of that part of the human race of which
they are more directly the offspring.
Homer is the great Pelasgian, Æschylus
is the great Greek, Job is the great
Arab, Isaias is the great Hebrew, Taci-

tus is the great Roman, Dante is the great Italian, Shakespeare is the great Englishman, Bossuet is the great Frenchman. And what is Jesus Christ? Neither Hebrew, nor Greek; neither ancient, nor modern. He is a man, or rather He is the man. In the others you do not find human nature in its fulness: you meet with a limit; in Jesus Christ you meet no limit.

And remark, that this universality does not imply the absence of individuality. For what individuality was ever so manifest, so sharply defined? Who ever spoke of Himself in such a tone of authority? Where is a more complete independence to be found? On whom is He dependent? Not on the multitude who cheer Him, not on His disciples, not on His century, not on the ideas and the customs in the midst of which He lives. None can claim to have been his master. It is by the sublimity even of His individuality that He attains to that singular universality. Moses is a Jew in his thoughts, his feelings, his manners, and his habits, even more than in his origin. Socrates

never raised himself above the Greek
type.   Mahomet was an Arab.   La
Fontaine and Molière are French to
such a degree, that the English have as
much trouble in understanding them as
the French have in appreciating Goethe.
All these great men have something in
them that is local and transient, which
cannot be understood beyond the mountain or the ocean, which cannot be
everywhere imitated ; something which
dies with the age, which springs up
again sometimes in another age, but
again to pass away by a strange vicissi-
tude, which shows that they are but
men, although the greatest among
men.   In Jesus Christ there is nothing
of this sort : His physiognomy shows
no   such   limits.   Human   nature
is there, but without anything to cir-
cumscribe it.   He is the universal
model proposed for universal imitation.
All copy Him : the child, the maiden,
the mother, the old man—all, whatever
their condition, whatever their age,
come to Him, to find consolation and
strength : the poor, as well as the rich,
the prisoner in his dungeon, and the

king upon his throne. To no purpose
are fresh actors brought on the scene
by the progress of the world and of
civilization : Jesus Christ is a stranger
to none—not to the Greek, although he
cared little for philosophy, not to the
Roman, though he may never have
gained a battle ; not to the barbarian of
the fourth century, nor to the polished
citizen of the nineteenth century, although their ideas, their habits, and
manners are so wholly dissimilar. He
has been adored by the Red-skins of
America, by the negroes of Africa, by
Brahmins of India ; and this adoration
has created in them virtues as pure,
and the same as those which sprang up
in the degenerate Romans of the Lower
Empire : His character so embraces all,
touches the sympathies of all, appears
to be within reach of all, is imitated by
all, in all times, though never equalled!

It would be unnecessary to repeat of
His influence what we have said of His
moral beauty and His individuality.
It follows as a matter of course. His
influence has no limit, either in time or
in space. It has no bounds anywhere,

in any direction. Above all, no age
has escaped from it. The human race
progresses, it presses forward rapidly,
like a messenger running in hot haste.
It blesses and hails on its path the geniuses which arise to carry the torch before it. Then very soon it leaves these
geniuses behind. The philosophy of
Plato was once good, but it no longer
serves our purpose ; the science of Newton was wonderful, but it has been
outstripped. The geology of Cuvier
effected a revolution, but it has disappeared. The human race advances.
Kindle fresh torches ! Hippocrates,
Archimedes, Copernicus, Galileo, La-
voisier, Montgolfier—all have been left
behind ; but not Jesus Christ. "Jesus
Christ," says M. Renan, "will never
be left behind." *

It is the glory, but at the same time
the weakness, of great masters that
their genius inspires them to dictate
formulas which become starting points
for further progress. And thus they
create disciples who cause them to be
forgotten. Although we may be very

* Renan, " Vie de Jésus."

inferior to Socrates and Plato, to Cicero
and Seneca, yet we know a thousand
truths of which they were ignorant.
We see a great many more which would
have astonished Bossuet, Newton, or
Pascal. "But," as Parker very well
says, "eighteen centuries have passed
since the tide of humanity rose so high
in Jesus : what man, what sect, what
church, has mastered His thoughts,
comprehended His method, and so fully
applied it to life ? Let the world answer in its cry of anguish. Men have
parted His raiment among them, cast
lots for His seamless coat ; but that
spirit which toiled so manfully in a
world of sin and death, which did, and
suffered, and overcame the world—is
that found, possessed, understood ?" *
After eighteen centuries it is unex-
hausted, and inexhaustible.

It even seems that the more the
human race progresses, the more striking becomes the influence of Jesus
Christ. On each new horizon it throws
a sudden ray of light : for each new

* Theodore Parker, " Discourse of Matters per-
taining to Religion," p. 226. Chapman, 1846.

want it provides a remedy till then unknown. What marvels are there not which the Christians of the first century never suspected, yet of which we are compelled to say—they were present to His mind. And what marvels that we do not perceive, of which our descendants will say—He foresaw these also.

And at the same time that it extends thus through centuries, and is renewed with every advance of civilization, this influence of Jesus Christ loses nothing of its intensity. After the lapse of eighteen centuries it masters souls as it did on the first day. "The story of the conquests of Alexander," said Napoleon, "kindles our enthusiasm : here is a conqueror who conquers and appropriates to Himself, not one nation only, but the entire human race. What a miracle ! The human soul, with all its powers, is absorbed in the existence of Jesus Christ." *

If, after having sought in vain the limits of His moral beauty, of His Individuality, and of His influence, we

* "Conversations de Napoléon à Sainte-Hélène, avec le Général Bertrand."

now contemplate His mind, we find ourselves face to face with a phenomenon
of the same order, but still more wonderful. The mind of Jesus Christ is
not only superior to every human mind,
as we demonstrated above : it has no
resemblance to other minds. It con-
tains something that is incomprehensible, beyond our gaze.

You are familiar with the Gospel.
Have you remarked in its pages, which
contain a doctrine at once so pure, and
so profound, and yet so definite, a
strange sort of light, which resembles,
but is not, obscurity ; for obscurity
could not be conceived in this lofty and
vigorous mind : a light so different from
the light of reason that some have called
it folly, though that cannot be ; otherwise in the course of centuries mankind
would have demonstrated its absurdity ;
a light, which certainly is light, for it
shines very brightly, although its source
is concealed from us ; a light, which not
knowing how to define, we have called
mystery—that is to say, the incomprehensible, the unapproachable ?

It may be said that clouds seem to

float around these light-giving discourses of the Gospel. From time to
time we meet with obscure words ; obscure, not from the absence of light,
but rather by reason of its intensity.
And the proof is, that the greatest
geniuses, the friends and foes of religion
alike, have studied them for eighteen
centuries, and its friends have not succeeded in understanding them, nor its
foes in overthrowing them. An Origen,
an Augustine, a Thomas of Aquin, a
Bossuet, a Leibnitz, a Pascal, have contemplated these mysterious pages with
the same attention which had discovered the laws of thought, and the
course of the stars ; and they have declared that they did not understand
them, but that these mysteries, which
in themselves they could not compre-
hend, enabled them to see and understand all else. At the same time another race arose, great minds also, skil-
ful in seizing the weak side of things,
in unraveling sophisms, and in casting
ridicule and contempt, and they under-
took to show that these pages contained
nothing but contradictions, follies, and

obscurities ; but they succeeded no better. In fact, had they proved their assertion, Christianity would have died out in contempt. So that after eighteen centuries of keenest discussion, these pages hold good, unfathomed, and, consequently, unfathomable.

Such is the phenomenon. It is unique. Search the books of philosophers : where will you find the unfathomable ? You will find obscurity, but obscurity is but one proof of weakness. You will sometimes find contradictions, and you will be able to give the proof of it. But the incomprehensible, the unapproachable, you will never find. A man cannot be incomprehensible by wishing to be so, nor can he impose a mystery on the world at his pleasure. What one mind conceives, another can conceive, and though it is given to genius to be the first to attain to certain heights, it cannot rise so high but that others rise also, or at least follow in its train. Genius resembles the eagle, who takes her little ones on her wings and soars with them to the sun, whither they would be incapable of

ᘓ going without help. ⌊Jesus Christ alone
cannot be followed. He is seen soaring
over the heights, like the geniuses of
this world. Like them He has elevation, depth, fertility : like them, and
more than they, He pours down floods
of human light. Then suddenly He
rises higher ; He enters the cloud ; He
is lost in an intense, impenetrable light,
where none can follow Him.

It is this which makes the Gospel an
incomparable book. Light, now ap-
proachable, now unapproachable, min-
gling in the same discourse, enraptures
you at one moment, and at another
strikes you to the ground. At times
you feel your footing no longer secure,
but there is no fear ; you know with
whom you are mounting. Those who
can no longer see, adore. And then
this intense impenetrable light sheds
such beautiful rays. It is like the sun,
at which one cannot gaze without being
dazzled, but one can see the rays which
come from it, and which enlighten the
world and give it all its beauty.

These characteristics, which have so
little that is human in them, though

they belong to a nature so humanly beautiful, have forcibly struck all those observers who, particularly during the last two centuries, have begun to study Jesus Christ, no longer as formerly by the exterior of His Being, but by its interior. Rousseau in the eighteenth century, after only a very hasty glance, let his admiration find vent in this celebrated saying, " If the life and death of Socrates are those of a sage, the life and the death of Jesus are those of a God." * In our days, Napoleon had but to fix his eagle glance for one moment on Jesus Christ to give utterance to a yet more beautiful expression —" I know something about men, and I tell you that Jesus Christ was no mere man ! " † Goethe, the most universal and mighty, but at the same time the most pagan of modern poets, calls Christ " the divine man, the saint, the type and model of all men." ‡

* Rousseau, " Emile, ou l'Education," livre vi.

† Beauterne, " Sentiments de Napoléon sur le Christianisme."

‡ Goethe, "Entretiens avec Eckerman." 3me vol.

In America, Channing, who took such pains to destroy the idea of the Divinity of Jesus Christ in the minds of his contemporaries, was obliged to confess that He presented features which the presence of mere human nature could not explain. " I believe," he said, " Jesus Christ to be a more than human being." And he adds, " Those who suppose Him not to have existed before His birth" (that is to say, who deny His Divinity) " do not regard Him as a mere man. They always separate Him by broad distinctions from other men. They consider Him as enjoying a communion with God, and as having received gifts, endowments, aids, lights from Him, granted to no other, and as having exhibited a spotless purity which is the highest distinction of Heaven. All admit, and joyfully admit, that Jesus Christ, by his greatness and goodness, throws all other human attainments into obscurity." *

After all, even those who in this century have looked most closely, though

* Channing, "The Imitableness of Christ's Character."

with hostility, into the character of Jesus Christ, who have declared themselves His avowed enemies,—Strauss in Germany, Parker in America, Renan in France,—have been forced to make very significant confessions. " Christ," says Strauss, " has not been followed by any who surpass Him, nor even by any who can attain after Him, and through Him, to the same perfection of religious life. Never, at any time, will it be possible to rise above Him, nor to imagine any who should even be equal with Him." * Parker is yet more explicit. The Divinity which manifests itself through the beautiful human character of Jesus Christ seems to show itself to him. " Jesus pours out a doctrine beautiful as the light, sublime as heaven, true as God. The Philosophers, the Poets, the Prophets, the Rabbis, He rises above them all. And yet Nazareth was no Athens where Philosophy breathed in the circumambient air ; it had neither Porch nor Lyceum : not even a school of the Prophets.

---

* Strauss, "Du passager et du permanent dans le Christianisme." Altona, 1839, p. 127.

There is God in the heart of this youth ! " *

Such is Parker's conclusion. Listen to that of M. Renan. " Rest now in Thy glory, Thou noble pioneer. Thy work is accomplished. . . . A thousand times more living, a thousand times more loved since Thy death than during the days of Thy earthly life, Thou shalt so become the corner-stone of the human edifice that to take away Thy name from this world would be to shake it to its very foundations. Between Thee and God there is no longer any distinction. Thou hast completely overcome death : take possession of Thy kingdom. Ages of adorers will follow Thee thither by the royal road which Thou hast traced." †

Let us gather up the result. All observers, even the most careless and the most antagonistic, manifest an involuntary veneration, a growing admiration for the spotless purity, for the moral perfection, and for the beauty of

* Theodore Parker, " Discourse of Matters pertaining to Religion," p. 220. Chapman, 1846.

† Renan, " Vie de Jesus."

this unequaled character. It seems to be more and more felt and admitted that He is the holiest amongst the holy in the history of our race, the greatest and the best that has ever trodden this earth. He is acknowledged to be so great, so good, and after the lapse of eighteen centuries so living, that the deepest thinkers involuntarily ask themselves if He is man, and the question arises in the minds of His enemies in spite of themselves. Now, that the question should arise, that the doubt should spring up of itself, that it should require an effort to put aside a question which does not arise in the case of any other man—is not this a presumption, and as it were, a first proof of his Divinity ?

4

CHAPTER III.

The miracles of Jesus Christ.—How they must be
    studied, and how their truth and beauty
    may be verified.

BUT let us advance, and plunge
boldly into the depths of this incomparable subject.   At present we are but at
the threshold.   If Jesus Christ is in
truth God, how could He be satisfied to
allow His Divinity to manifest Itself
through His human intellect, His human heart, His human will?   Could
such a twilight satisfy us?   He intended
to claim from us an absolute faith; it
was necessary, then, that He should
give us proofs of His Divinity proportioned to the greatness of the adoration
He exacted from us.   And since God,
who has given us such splendid gifts,
has not permitted us to control the laws
of creation; since through force of
genius we can pass through tempests,
but are not able to calm them; since

we do not know how to bring our dead to life again, even those who are dearest to us, it was necessary that Jesus Christ should do it, and that, after having permitted us to have a glimpse of His Divinity through the veil of His Humanity, as a light that is too brilliant is softened under a crystal globe, there should be some rays of extremely brilliant light, some of those sovereign acts which remove all doubt from men of good will, and compel them to fall down in adoration.

And this Jesus Christ has done. Remember the cure of the man born blind. Remember Lazarus raised to life again. Remember Mount Thabor or the Sea of Galilee. If these facts are true, are they not in some sort an outburst of the Divinity?

But nevertheless it is not my intention at present to insist on the historical certitude of these facts. We wish to know if Jesus Christ is God. We may follow two methods. The first is to prove that He worked real miracles—that is to say, that He performed actions beyond the powers of human nature to perform,

SACRED HEART RETREAT
NEWBURG ROAD
LOUISVILLE, - KY.

and making an exception to all the laws of creation ; that He performed them often, frequently, thousands of times ; that He performed them in the full blaze of the midday sun, in the streets, in the public places, in the presence of His friends, before immense crowds, under the eager and malicious gaze of His enemies ; that there is no natural manner of explaining these miracles, which His contemporaries never called in question ; and that all the physical, metaphysical, and scientific impossibilities which are alleged against them are of absolutely no avail. This is the first method, the method adopted by the ancient apologists, who carried it to perfection.

There is a second method, more beautiful, and more according to the spirit of our work. It is to show that Jesus accomplished these actions, whatever they may be, in a superhuman manner. It is to look at them, no longer as regards their surroundings, but in themselves ; to unfold them as we unfold a flower, that their perfume may be breathed forth ; and to recognize there

under another form the true character
of Jesus Christ, His great and piercing
mind, His sublime heart, His stupen-
dous virtue, and, as it were, a higher im-
press of His divinity. None but God
could have done such acts; but still
more, none but God would have done
them as He did them. This is the
second method. We prefer it to the
other, and it is the one we shall employ.
To those who are seeking, and are in
doubt, it gives less handle to the sub-
tleties of the intellect; it opens a vast
horizon to the intuitions of the heart;
it appeals to the conscience, the true
judge in such matters; and for all these
reasons it is wonderfully adapted to
make us take a new and decisive step in
the knowledge of Jesus Christ.

We sometimes ask, whence arose the
popularity of the Saviour and the success of His work : and we are tempted
to reply that it was owing to His miracles, which, in demonstrating that He
was superior to nature, brought all men
to His feet. This answer is at best very
incomplete. Had He performed no miracles, Jesus Christ would none the less

have brought the world to His feet; and, on the other hand, had they been multiplied a thousand-fold, and been yet more striking, if He had not displayed in such acts the moral beauty, the gentleness, the discretion, the infinite tenderness which He did display, instead of attracting souls to Him, He would have alarmed and repelled them. " Supernatural power," says a profound observer, "was not invariably connected in the minds of the ancients with God and goodness; it was supposed to be in the gift of evil spirits as well as good; it was regarded with horror in as many cases as with reverence." And, indeed, when wielded by Christ, the first impression which it produced upon those who witnessed it was one of alarm and distress. Men were not so much disposed to admire or adore as to escape precipitately from the presence of one so formidable. The Gadarenes prayed Christ to depart out of their coasts. Even Peter made the same petition, and that at a time when he knew too much of his Master utterly to misapprehend His character and purpose.

It appears, then, that these supernatural powers freely used were calculated to hinder Christ's plan almost as much as to further it. The sense of being in the hands of a Divine Teacher is in itself elevating and beneficial ; but the close proximity of an overwhelming force crushes freedom and reason. Had Christ used supernatural power without restraint, as his countrymen seemed to expect of Him, and as ancient prophecy seemed to justify them in expecting, when it spoke of the Messiah ruling the nations with a rod of iron, and breaking them in pieces like a potter's vessel, we cannot imagine that any redemption would have been wrought for man. The power would have neutralized instead of seconding the wisdom and goodness which wielded it. So long as it was present it would have fettered and frozen the faculties of those on whom it worked, so that the legislation which it was used to introduce would have been placed on the same footing as the commands of a tyrant ; and, on the other hand, as soon as it was removed, the legislation and it would have passed into oblivion together. . . . Christ avoided this result. He imposed upon himself a strict restraint in the use of his supernatural powers. He adopted the principle that he was not sent to destroy men's lives, but to save them, and rigidly abstained in practise from inflicting any kind of damage or harm. In this course he persevered so steadily that it became generally understood. Every one knew that this *King,* whose royal pretensions were so prominent, had an absolutely unlimited patience, and that he would endure the keenest criticism, the bitterest and most malignant personal attacks. Men's mouths were opened to discuss his claims and character with entire freedom. So far from regarding him with that excessive fear which might have prevented them from receiving his doctrine intelligently, they learnt gradually to treat him, even while they acknowledged his extraordinary power, with a reckless animosity which they would have been afraid to show towards an ordinary enemy. With curious inconsistency they openly charged him with being leagued with the devil ; in other words, they acknowledged that he was capable of boundless mischief, and yet they were so little afraid of him that they were ready to provoke him to use his whole power against themselves. The truth was, that they believed him to be disarmed by his own deliberate resolution, and they judged rightly. He punished their malice only by verbal reproofs, and they gradually gathered courage to attack the life of one whose miraculous powers they did not question.*

These beautiful and very original views of a Protestant author claim our attention. They light up one side of the wonderful character of Jesus Christ. It is not only in the domain of science that conquests are made in our times, but also in the domain of criticism. Here is one. This voluntary disarming of Christ ; this discretion, infinite in wisdom as in love ; this formidable power known by all to be in His hands,

* " Ecce Homo. Christ's Credentials," 4th ed., p. 31.

and which yet strikes terror into no one ; this conviction, become general little by little, that He is incapable of abusing it ; and these crowds, emboldened so far as to attack the life of Him, whose miraculous power they do not question ;—all this, I repeat, is original, and full of deep thought, and throws on the true character of Jesus a ray of light at once gentle and striking.

This miraculous power which He wielded so royally, which He held back so mightily, so that no provocation, no danger, no treason, no contempt could induce Him to use it in His own defense, seemed to escape from His control when there was a question of doing good to others. Let Him meet the poor, or the sick, and swift as lightning this divine power escaped from His heart in acts of love. Sometimes it would almost seem as though He were no longer the master of it, as in the incomparable history of the poor woman who approached Him humbly from behind, saying, "If I can but touch the hem of His garment I shall be cured." On certain occasions He even gave way to tears, and groanings, and unwonted trouble which bore witness to the intensity of His love. Who does not recall the impulse of mercy which touched Him at Nain, by the side of the bier of the only son, and the sorrowing mother ? Who can forget His deep emotion so mastered, when He raises the daughter of Jairus to life ? How shall we forget the unwonted agitation which He manifests at the tomb of Lazarus ! But neither these troubles, nor these tender impulses of the most sensitive of all hearts, could penetrate the tranquil region where dwelt His miraculous power. As He is unmoved under the shadow of the highest mysteries, so He preserves His self-possession when working the greatest miracles. "He raises the dead to life in the same way that He performs the most ordinary action : He speaks as a master to those who sleep an eternal sleep, and we feel that He is the God of the living, and of the dead : never more calm than when He performs the greatest acts." *

* Massillon, "Sermon sur la Divinité de Jésus Christ."

By degrees, through this sublime power, and still more through the sublime use that He made of it, the brow of Jesus was crowned with a new halo. " This reserve in the use of His supernatural power," concludes the English author just quoted, " is the masterpiece of Christ. It is a moral miracle, added to a physical miracle." This repose joined to majesty, and I will add, this laying down His power where there is so much power, renders Him the noblest figure that has ever been presented to human imagination.

But Jesus did not only enrapture the multitude by this miraculous power manifested in love, and in an impulse of the most tender, most merciful, most delicate, and most intense love, joined to the most marvelous forgetfulness of self : His lofty intellect also revealed itself. He did not content Himself with healing, He went beyond the body to the soul. To say the truth, He never occupied Himself but with souls. It is evident that Jesus saw the diseases of the soul through the diseases of the body. He beheld the sore point in the soul, which had produced the like in the body, and to that He applied His great and benevolent power. His miracles were not merely extraordinary acts which excite wonder but convey no instruction ; nor were they merely acts of compassion and kindness : they were something deeper—acts in which all His saving power was displayed. The Saviour of souls, the Redeemer, was living and visible through these miracles. Thus before He performed any miracle He desired that the divine energies of the soul should be awakened and united to Him. " Dost thou believe ? " He said ; or " Wilt thou be saved ? " And again, " If you could but believe ! " He would only act when the infirm soul had at least endeavored to turn to the Physician.

What tongue can tell the tact of this being to whom all souls were revealed, whilst exercising this noble ministry ! What touching reserve ! What delicacy not to humiliate one whose wounds He saw, above all not to betray him to those who stood around ! What hints sufficient to enlighten the sufferer without disclosing his state to others. " Go in peace, sin no more ! . . . . Many sins are forgiven you, because you have loved much." And a thousand other words of tenderest tact and of divine gentleness. Consequently He could go nowhere without being surrounded by all those who had had a share in His kindness—sick whom He had cured, lepers whom He had made clean, possessed whom He had snatched from the power of the demon, a crowd of sinners, men and women, whom he had saved from vice and degradation by an act of power which did not humble them.

When we see the way in which these things took place, and then think of the prejudices of our modern sceptics, of the commissions of doctors, chemists, physicians which they require to verify a miracle, we cannot help smiling as at a blind man who should reason about light. It was not the miracle which entranced the crowd, so much as the way in which it was done. " It was neither for His miracles, nor for the beauty of His doctrine, that Christ was worshipped. Nor was it for His winning personal character, nor for the persecutions He endured, nor for His martyrdom. It was for the inimitable unity which all these things made when taken together. In other words it was for this, that He whose power and greatness, as shown in His miracles, were overwhelming, denied Himself the use of His power, treated it as a slight thing, walked among men as though He were one of them, relieved them in distress, taught them to love each other, bore with undisturbed patience a perpetual hail-storm of calumny ; and when His enemies grew fiercer, continued still to endure their attacks in silence, until petrified and bewildered with astonishment, men saw Him arrested and put to death with torture, refusing steadfastly to use in His own behalf the power He conceived He held for the benefit of others. It was the combination of greatness and self-sacrifice which won their hearts, the mighty powers held under a mighty control, the unspeakable condescension, the *Cross of Christ.*" *

* " Ecce Homo. Christ's Credentials,",4th ed., p. 46.

To this end there was no need of a
commission of physiologists or physicians ; the world had never witnessed
anything like it.   Man had never even
imagined so lofty a character.

" They saw Him hungry, though they
believed Him able to turn the stones
into bread ; they saw His royal pretensions spurned, though they believed
that He could in a moment take into
His hand all the kingdoms of the world,
and the glory of them ; they saw His
life in danger ; they saw Him at last
expire in agonies, though they believed
that, had He so willed it, no danger
could harm Him, and that, had He
thrown Himself from the topmost pin-
nacle of the Temple, He would have
been softly received in the arms of
ministering angels.   Witnessing His
sufferings, and convinced by the miracles they saw Him work, that they were
voluntarily endured, men's hearts were
touched, and pity for weakness blend-
ing strangely with wondering admiration of unlimited power ; an agitation
of gratitude, sympathy, and astonishment, such as nothing else could ever

excite, sprang up in them ; and when, turning from His deeds to His words, they found this very self-denial which had guided His own life prescribed as the principle which should guide theirs, gratitude broke forth in joyful obedience, self-denial produced self-denial, and the Law and Law-Giver together were enshrined in their inmost hearts for inseparable veneration." *

* " Ecce Homo.   Christ's Credentials," 4th ed., p. 51.

CHAPTER IV.

The perfect holiness of Jesus Christ.—The spotless and absolute perfection of His life.

THESE last words lead us to consider
a new feature, the most beautiful perhaps in the physiognomy of Jesus
Christ. I mean His perfect sanctity,
the spotless and absolute perfection of
His life in the midst of a world filled
with sins and uncleanness. We have
already contemplated His mind, His
heart, His will, His actions : let us go
one step beyond, let us look into His
conscience.

Pascal, after contemplating it, was
as it were dazzled, and wrote these
words of sublime incoherence : "Jesus
Christ was gentle, patient, thrice holy
in the sight of God, terrible to demons,
sinless."

This, in fact, is the divine feature,
and all that we have hitherto consid-

ered fades in presence of the sanctity of Jesus Christ.

But that which strikes me most in this unique sanctity is, not the marvelous efflorescence of all the virtues, each attaining its ideal in a harmonious group :—No, there is something more delicate and more human that I seek in Him, and that I do not find. I seek regret for sin, the sad remembrance of former faults, and also the holy tears of repentance, the firm resolutions of amendment—all this divine side of the soul and of the human conscience. This is what I look for, and what I do not find.

Strange ! I find in Him the highest summits of perfection : I do not find that on which it rests. What does this mean ? Who will explain to me this mystery ?

St. John declared, "If any say he has no sin, he deceives himself, and the truth is not in him." St. Paul called himself "the chief of sinners, a man sold to sin, and in whom dwelt no good thing." M. de Maistre said, "I do not know what the heart of a villain is like.

I only know that of an upright man, and it is frightful." Every sound conscience must use this language. Picture to yourself a saint, let him be the greatest saint, put these words on his lips, "I am holy, there is no sin in me;" at once he falls from his pedestal, and the conscience of man turns against him in anger, and strips him of his crown. Man may be proud that he can no more realize his dream of holiness than he can his other dreams; that he stops powerless before his ideal of good, as before his ideal of beauty; and whether he spreads a masterpiece on his canvas, or whether his noble heart in self-sacrifice begets some heroic act, dissatisfied with himself he will say sorrowfully, I shall never reach it.

Yet there is one exception. There is a man who once said, I am holy; a man who said, "Which of you shall convince me of sin?" There is a man, the humblest, the purest, the most clear-sighted of all, who said, "Be ye holy, as I am holy;" and yet this strange affirmation, repeated twenty times, has detracted nothing from the glory

that encircles Him. And not only
throughout his entire life is there not a
single moment of hesitation visible in
the calm assertion of His absolute perfection, but this man who has ever the
liveliest perception of sin, who has a
thirst for the conversion of the whole
human race, who passes His life in calling all men to repentance,—who, while
touching the eyes of the blind, and the
limbs of the paralyzed, seems to be
moved by their sins alone : "Go in
peace, your sins are forgiven you. . . .
Go, sin no more ! "—this man, I say,
never betrays the faintest suspicion that
He Himself may stand in need of pardon. Never does He strike His breast,
never does He shed one single tear of
repentance, neither at the Garden of
Olives, nor at Golgotha : never does He
regret a single thought, nor a single
act. He says to His disciples, " *You*,
when you pray, shall say, 'Our Father
who art in heaven, forgive us our tres-
passes.'" He Himself never prays
thus. Man like us, acting like a man,
living, suffering, dying like a man : I
will say more, tempted like a man,

surrounded with sin, having the most
intense horror of it, thirsting for the
salvation of the whole human race ;—
never do we see Him concerned about
His own salvation. He has a pure and
spotless conscience ; a conscience of sublime peace and serenity, never clouded
by a shadow of regret, or remorse, or
fear, and the pure breath from His
bosom, the ineffable brightness of His
glance, the divine calm of His soul,
seem to say ever, "Holy, holy, holy :
innocent, separated from sinners."

This conviction that Jesus had of the
perfect and absolute purity of His soul,
all His contemporaries have also, even
those who are the nearest to Him. Or
rather, the more familiarly they live
with Him, the more intense and boundless becomes their admiration. From
the first they were struck with an instantaneous conviction of the perfection
of their Master, and that conviction
gained strength every day. They are
prostrate at His feet, and thither they
drag the world with them. Not that
their enthusiasm finds vent in praises, in
words of admiration for His virtues : this

does not enter into their minds. They relate humbly, simply, without phrases, without commentary, what they have seen. But what they have seen is of such an order that, on reading the Gospel, the words of Pascal in their searching power rise involuntarily to the mind : " Jesus Christ was humble, patient, thrice holy in the sight of God, sinless."

Even His enemies shared this impression. Recognizing with the unerring instinct of hatred that no fault was compatible with the part He had assigned Himself, they are always watching Him, and laying snares for Him. As a traveler belated on a winter's night is followed by a troop of wolves, if He make a false step He is lost : thus Jesus passed His life, surrounded by Pharisees who seek to surprise Him in an imperfect or culpable act or word, and the proof that they could not succeed is, that in the end they have recourse to violence. He, always pure and gentle, always calm, beaming with inward peace, only replies to all their stratagems by this word of sovereign holiness : "Which of you convinceth me of sin ?" None had said it before Him, and none has dared to say it since.

And He does not address this challenge only to His enemies in Jerusalem : He addresses it to mankind in all countries, in all ages. He has made His Church to rest on this word. This is its foundation of granite. Its corner-stone is the diamond of the spotlesss purity of Jesus. Suppose, indeed, that a deception or a sin were to be discovered in the life of Jesus Christ—one of those faults of which there are thousands in our lives —the Church would vanish, and nothing would remain of this majestic edifice in which so many virtues have blossomed in the sunlight of the virtues of Jesus. It is an unique fact, and it raises Jesus Christ to a height immeasurably above the greatest men of the world. For which of them has been without sin ? Which of them has given his immaculate purity as the basis of a work of eighteen centuries ? Which has so identified his life with moral beauty that to depart from it is to depart from good, and to copy it is to attain good ? In this respect Jesus has no equal, no rival. He stands alone, and by the single fact of His spotless purity, He appears to us in the midst of other men as in a sublime solitude.

Must we add that the holiness of Jesus is not purely negative ? That which characterizes it is, not only exemption from all sin, but the perfection of every virtue. He has every virtue, and in Him each virtue so attains its full development, so perfectly fulfils its ideal, producing flower, and fruit, and perfume in such rich abundance, that great souls with all their efforts will but follow Him at a distance, without ever approaching Him. And although each virtue exists in Him in its full and absolute perfection, it is not prejudicial to the contrary virtue : it rather calls it forth. So that in Him we never see one virtue alone : there are always two absolutely opposite virtues, one as beautiful as the other, and from them spring the most unexpected contrasts, which blend at last in perfect harmony, as we have seen in studying the qualities of

His mind and heart. Who, for example, was more stern than Jesus Christ? Yet who was more tender? Who ever had a greater conviction of His intrinsic glory? Yet who was humbler? "This combination of the spirit of humanity in its lowliest, tenderest form, with the consciousness of unrivaled and divine glories, is," said Channing, "the most wonderful distinction of this wonderful character." *
Just now we were admiring His innocence and purity; but where shall we find a penitent who was more austere? Who ever knew the misery of mankind as He did? but who has loved men more? who has despised them less? Who has expected more from them? "As for me," says M. Guizot, "nothing strikes me more in the Gospel than this twofold character of severity and love, of austere purity and tender sympathy, which appears and triumphs uniformly in the acts and in the words of Christ." †

* Channing, "Discourse on the Character of Christ."

† Guizot, "Méditations sur l'Essence de la Religion chrétienne."

In short, take all the virtues, the beauties of soul the most opposite and contradictory in appearance. Name one, you will see another spring up: and whilst you are considering which is the more beautiful, you will see them blend in so perfect a proportion, in so pure a harmony, that you will be transported with delight.

And there is no break or effort. There are none of those moments where the man appears, nor are there any of those moments in which a man rises above himself by a violent effort which does him honor, but which cannot last. He rises without effort to the summit of the highest virtues. Or rather He has not to rise: He is there as in perfect naturalness, in peculiar sympathy. I call it peculiar, because this naturalness and this simplicity constitute His true originality. John the Baptist is certainly one of the greatest souls that have ever appeared. This great giant of penance arrests our attention and fills us with emotion. But there is nothing original in him. He continues the prophetic type: he resembles Elias and Eliseus : his holiness is of the same order. Christ is quite different. No camel's hair, no wild honey, no austerities to excite our fear. All is plain, simple, and ordinary : but if you look closely you will perceive a virtue which with the greatest ease surpasses all other virtues—an intense depth of humility, detachment, self-denial, contempt for the world, charity for men, union with God, which appears trifling at the first glance, but which soon makes those despair who try to approach it. These qualities play the part in the moral order which simplicity, sobriety, good taste, and exquisite beauty that characterize the greatest geniuses of Greece, play in the intellectual order. To write like them we fancy we have but to mend our pen, and we very soon learn, throwing it aside in vexation, what it costs to arrive at this naturalness.

As, moreover, suffering is the touchstone of moral perfection, it is not spared Him. Every trial is brought to bear on Him, in order to make His virtues more resplendent. He had said, *Blessed are the poor !* and He is exposed naked on a cross, but there is no change in the serenity of His countenance. He had said, *Blessed are the meek,*—and He was bound to a column, inhumanly scourged, buffeted, insulted, but He uttered no complaint. He had said, *Blessed are the merciful,*—and when Judas betrayed Him with a kiss, when Peter denied Him, when the executioners spit in His face, He has but one word, one look, one prayer, the word of pardon and of love. He had said, *Blessed are they who suffer persecution for justice,*—and after He has given everything to the world, His mind, His heart, His life, receiving in exchange suffering, and the infamy of the cross, He is thrilled with joy. Ah ! it is a grand thing to do good in this poor world, and not to ask a recompense. We bend the knee before those, who, forgetting self, sacrifice themselves, and before those, happier still, who are forgotten by those whom they have most loved. But to be hated by them, to be persecuted by them, to do the greatest possible good, to give one's whole life to men—and the purest, the most elevated of all lives, and to have no reward, to reap but ingratitude, to sink beneath the weight of one's benefactions, and so to be happy—never has there been anything greater on earth. Yes ! I throw a veil over the divinity of Jesus Christ. I look at Him on His cross, having done good by the impulse of the purest love that ever existed, having realized it at the price of the greatest sufferings, and having been paid by ingratitude, and I say that there is the sublime height of moral beauty and virtue. What was the death of Socrates beside this death ? What was Plato's ideal of the just man suffering, compared to this reality ? True indeed is the saying of Rousseau, "If the life and the death of Socrates are those of a sage, the life and the death of Jesus are those of a God."

If I seek the cause of a virtue so high, so constant, so sustained in life and in death, so simple, yet so natural—in one word so perfect : if, after following the course of this grand river I try to reach its source ; if, in order that I may understand the exterior man who fills me with wonder, I endeavor to penetrate into the interior man, what do I find? It would seem as though in the innermost sanctuary of His soul, there were some unseen guest who never leaves Him. " He never leaves me alone," He said when speaking of this guest. Whilst men keep silence to gather His words, He keeps silence also, but it is to listen to Him. He converses with this unseen guest as with a confidant. He contemplates His face, invisible to all except to Him. It is an intimate communion with another, so that in solemn moments, like a man thinking aloud, He lets words escape Him which are but detached fragments of the mysterious colloquy which is going on within. " I knew well," He says at the tomb of Lazarus, "that Thou hearest me always." And in the Garden of Olives, " If it be possible, let this chalice pass from me ! But not as I will, but as Thou wilt." And on the cross, " Why hast Thou forsaken me ? " It would seem as though He had another self, above Him, and yet His equal, whom He adores in silence, whom He loves

above all, by whom He is loved, and
with whom He lives in that tender unity
of which He says—"He and I are one."

Moreover, He makes no mystery of
this interior intimacy. He never tires
when He endeavors to make His disciples understand the ineffable relation
which unites Him to this unseen Being,
who to Him is more living, more present, more familiar, more visible than
the most beloved of His apostles. "My
Father," so He calls Him, "loves me."
"As my Father knows me, so I know
my Father. The words which I say to
you, I do not say of myself, I have
learnt them of my Father. . .My food
is to do the will of my Father. . . I and
my Father are one;" and many similar
expressions which we shall meet with
later.

But what then is this relation which
exists between Him and His Father :
this full and perpetual indwelling of
God in Him? Is it only the relation
that we ourselves have with God ; a
higher relation no doubt, but of the
same kind? Is it something different?
Who shall tell us?   Who knows except

He ? We proceed as we can—from what
we see to what we do not see : we con-
jecture, we catch a glimpse, but beyond
a certain point we see no further. If
God be there, let Him say so. We have
penetrated to the tabernacle. O God !
open it ; say if Thou art there ! O
Jesus ! Art Thou but a saint, a just
man, a man most tenderly, most deeply
united to God ? Is there anything
further ? Is there more ? Speak, oh
speak ! It is time that Thou shouldst
speak, and our hearts, prepared to listen,
will reply to Thy words by the silence
of adoration, and the joyous outpouring
of love.

6

CHAPTER V.

Jesus Christ plainly asserts His Divinity.—He
is the Son of God.

THIS great name of Son of Man, of
which we spoke above, which Jesus assumed continually, and which recurs
more than eighty times in the Gospel,
contained in itself a peculiar and startling revelation of His true nature.   For
whence could He have derived that
sublime peculiarity of being not only *a*
son of man, like all the descendants of
Adam, but of being *the* Son of Man, the
perfect man, in whom, and in whom
only, the human ideal is fulfilled ?
How is it that He alone has realized all
that is contained in the idea of man ?
And is it that on this account He knows
Himself to be, and calls Himself, the
Head of the Human race, which He,
and no other, can raise, heal and enlighten, on condition of its being united

to Him. "The Father has given Him power to do judgment, because He is *the Son of Man*." * "The *Son of Man* is come to save that which was lost." † " Except you eat the flesh of the *Son of Man*, and drink His blood, you shall not have life in you." ‡ "He that will be first among you shall be your serv- ant. Even as the *Son of Man* is not come to be ministered unto, but to min- ister, and to give His life a redemption to many." §

All these texts, and so many others which express either His supernatural elevation above the common level, or His touching condescension and volun- tary self-abasement in coming down to our fallen race, constitute, in my opinion, the vestibule, and as it were, the splendid portico through which we enter into the shrine of His Divinity.

But if He called Himself *Son of Man*, He called Himself also, and still more clearly, *Son of God*, His *only* Son, be- gotten of the Father before all ages, who had descended from Heaven, and

* John v. 27.   † Matth. xviii. 11.
‡ John vi. 54.   § Matth. xx. 27, 28.

was alone capable of reascending thither, and taking the human race with Him.

All who surrounded Him call Him the Son of God, without provoking in His humble soul the least surprise, or the least opposition. Peter fell on his knees, and said to Him, "Thou art the Christ, *the Son of the living God.*" *

Martha, "Lord, I believe that Thou art the Christ, *the Son of the living God,* who art come into this world." †

Thomas, after having touched the wounds of His feet and hands, "Thou art my Lord, and *my God.*" ‡ And all the Apostles, when He had calmed the tempest, "Truly Thou art *the Son of God.*" §

What does Christ reply ? Is He surprised ? Is He moved to grief and indignation at seeing the sacred and incommunicable name of God transferred to a creature ? Three years afterwards, when the people, carried away by the teaching and the miracles of Paul and Barnabas, threw themselves at their

* Matth. xvi. 16.   † John xi. 27.
‡ John xx. 28.   § Matth. xiv. 33.

feet to adore them, Paul was in-
dignant, Barnabas rent his garments,
and both Apostles exclaimed from the
sincerity of their hearts, "Brethren,
why do ye these things? We also
are mortals, men like unto you." Remember, too, the extreme careful-
ness of John the Baptist not to deceive
the people. He is always saying, " I
am not the Christ, I am not He whom
you look for." And who does not rec-
ollect the anger of Moses, and his noble
indignation, and the care to hide his
sepulchre in order not to take from God
the glory which belongs to Him. With
Jesus there is nothing of the sort. He
is called God, Son of God, true Son of
God, by all. Though so pure and
humble, so holy and wise, He calmly
lets Himself be called *Son of God*, and
adored as such.

And He not only accepts this title,
but He blesses and rewards those who
give it Him. " Blessed art thou," He
says to Simon, after he has confessed
the Divinity of Christ, "for it is not
flesh or blood,"—it is not prejudice,
ignorance, or passion, that have

prompted this confession—" My Father who is in heaven has revealed it to thee. And therefore I say to thee, Thou art Peter, and on this rock I will build my Church, and the gates of hell shall not prevail against it." *

Jesus Christ does yet more than simply accept this title, and bless those who give it Him ; for He assumes it Himself, and challenges those whom He wishes to save or heal to address Him by it. He says to the man who was born blind, " Dost thou believe in *the Son of God ?* " And the blind man, raising his newly opened eyes to Him, replies, " Who is He, that I may believe in Him ? " And Jesus continues, " Thou hast both seen Him, and it is He that talketh with thee." *Vidisti eum, et qui loquitur tecum ipse est.* And then the blind man falls at His feet and adores Him. *Et procidens adoravit eum.*†
Could He go farther ? If Jesus is not God, is not that a challenge to a crime ? And in order that we may not imagine that this name of Son is His only in the same way that we are called chil-

* Matth. xvi.   † John ix. 36-41.

dren of God by adoption, and great men
are called godlike, He asserts distinctly
that He is the *only Son* of God.   He
says to Nicodemus, "God so loved the
world, that He gave His only-begotten
Son"—*ut Filium suum unigenitum
daret*, the only son by nature—*unigenitum a Patre*, the son "who is in the
bosom of the Father, "*qui est in sinu
Patris.*

And He makes these words, which
He said to Nicodemus in the intimacy
of a private conversation, the ordinary
theme of His preaching in Jerusalem.
He affirms His divine, absolute, and
eternal filiation, His unity of essence
with the Father, in such terms that
the Jews, filled with indignation, stop
their ears, and take up stones to stone
Him.   And when Jesus said to them,
"Many good works I have shewed you
from My Father ; for which of those
works do you stone Me ?" they answered, "For a good work we stone
Thee not, but for blasphemy ; and because that Thou, being a man, makest
Thyself God." *

* John x. 32, 33,

He was arraigned before the courts, and neither prayers nor threats, nor supplications from those who were perplexed, nor the prospect of the penalty of death, can make Him forego His claim. "If thou be the Christ, tell us." And Jesus said, "If I shall tell you, you will not believe Me." The priests answered, "Art Thou then the Son of God?" "You say that I am."*

The High Priest was not satisfied with this reply. He insisted on putting the question with all possible distinctness, and investing it with the solemnity of religion. "I adjure Thee by the living God that Thou tell us if Thou be the Christ, the Son of God." And Jesus replied, "Thou hast said it."

He was taken to Pilate, and what was the accusation brought against Him? "We have a law; and according to the law He ought to die, because He made Himself the Son of God"—*quia Filium Dei se fecit.*†

The people acknowledged that it was for this, and for no other reason, that He suffered; and therefore, even in His

* Luke xxii. 67—70.   † John xix. 7.

agony, they insult Him with the cry, "If Thou be the Son of God, come down from the cross." *Si Filius Dei es, descende de cruce.**

Thus Jesus called Himself God, Son of God, true Son of God. He did not content Himself merely with accepting this title, with blessing and recompensing those who gave it to Him—He assumed it Himself, in private, in public, in the streets of Jerusalem, and before the tribunals. He died rather than renounce it. He died because He assumed it. On this point there is no ambiguity, for it is admitted by even the most advanced rationalists. "The expression *Son of God*," says M. Salvador, "was in ordinary use among the Hebrews to indicate a man of great wisdom, and great piety. *It was not in this sense that Christ made use of it : for then it would not have caused such a sensation.*" And he adds, "The question the people had raised was this : Did Jesus make Himself God ? Now the Council, judging that Jesus, son of Joseph, born in Bethlehem, had pro-

* Matth. xxvii. 40.

faned the name of God in arrogating it
to Himself, but a simple citizen, applied to Him the law against blasphemy, and pronounced sentence of
death." * Such is the fact, and certainly
it suggests matter for reflection.

But the logical intrepidity of this assertion is, I may dare to say so, still
more striking than its novelty, its bold-
ness, and ever increasing vehemence.
In fact, Jesus assumes all the titles of
God, Jesus claims all the homage due to
God, and, I may say, He exercises all the
powers of God. This, in fact, is the
main point ; for we may dispute about
a name, about the meaning of a Hebrew
expression, although under certain con-
ditions of clearness and precision, such
as we have just cited, discussion would
be very difficult. But this is not the
question. Jesus has not only assumed
the name of God, of the Son of God ;
but He has also assumed the offices and
acts, the necessary and sovereign attributes of the Divinity.

Let us first remark that when Christ
calls Himself God, He draws a clear dis-

* Vie de Jésus-Christ, t. ii., p. 217.

tinction between Himself and God the Father who sent Him, whose works He is come to do, to whose will He submits, to whom He prays, with whom He converses interiorly. *"My Father loves me. . . . My meat is to do the will of my Father. . . . I do always what is pleasing to my Father. . . . I will pray the Father. . . . O Father, I know that Thou hearest me always."*

There the distinction of persons is perfectly stated.

He draws the same clear distinction between Himself and the Holy Ghost, who rested on Him at His Baptism, whom He breathed upon His disciples, whom He promised to send to them as the spirit of truth and holiness, with the fulness of all gifts. *"I will ask the Father, and He will give you another Comforter . . . the Spirit of truth. I tell you the truth: it is expedient for you that I go : for if I go not, the Paraclete will not come to you : but if I go, I will send Him to you."*

Thus Jesus draws a clear distinction between Himself and the Father, and again between Himself and the Holy

Ghost. He never draws a distinction between Himself and the Son. He never speaks of the Son as of one different from Himself. He is the Son. He takes the name of the Son, and in a sense which implies nothing short of perfect and substantial equality with the Father and the Holy Ghost. Listen to this passage, at once so intelligible and mysterious, and meditate upon it : "I am the way, and the truth, and the life. No man cometh to the *Father* but by *me*. . . . Philip saith to Him : Lord, shew us the *Father*, and it is enough for us. Jesus saith to him : So long a time have I been with you, and have you not known me? Philip, he that seeth *me*, seeth the *Father* also. How sayest thou, Shew us the *Father* ? Do you not believe that *I am in the Father*, and *the Father in me* ? . . . Otherwise believe for the very works' sake. Amen, amen, I say to you, he that believeth in me, the works that I do, he also shall do, and greater than these shall he do : because I go to the Father : and whatsoever you shall ask the Father in my name that will I do : that *the Father* may be glorified *in the Son.* If you love me keep my commandments, and *I* will ask the *Father* and He shall give you *another* Paraclete, that He may abide with you for ever. *The Spirit of truth*, whom the world cannot receive, because it seeth Him not, nor knoweth Him. . . . If any one love me, he will keep my word, and my Father will love him, and *we* will come to him, and will make *our* abode with him." *

This passage reveals to us the three Persons of the Holy Trinity. We have the unity of nature and distinction of persons. And among these three Persons, Jesus is the Son. As such He affirms His real and conscious pre-existence before man existed—or rather before the world existed. "Verily, verily, I say to you, before Abraham was (began to be) I am." † And in the prayer of the Last Supper—"Father, glorify Thou me with the glory that I had with Thee before the world was." ‡ And hence all those wonderful and sublime expressions : I am the Light of the World. . . . I am come a Light into

* John xiv. 6—23.   † John viii. 58.
‡ John xvii. 5.

the world. . . . He who followeth me
walketh not in darkness. I am the Way,
the Truth, and the Life. . . . I am the
Beginning. I am the Resurrection and
the Life. I am the Living Bread that
came down from Heaven." . . . Expressions which would be those of a madman if they were not those of a God :
words which should have scorched His
lips, and He pronounces them with
divine calmness. Amidst declarations
so startling, there is not to be found in
Him the least thought of pride, ambition, or vanity. He speaks and acts
with the simplicity and superiority of
undeniable truth.

Not merely does He assume all the
titles which belong to God alone, but
consistently with this assumption He
does all the works of a God. He speaks
as God. "It was said to them of old
and *I* say unto you." *   He commands,
as God : "Go, teach all nations. . . .
teach them to observe all things whatsoever I have commanded you. And behold I am with you always, even to the
consummation of the world." †   He

* S. Matt. v. 21, 22.   † S. Matt. xxviii. 20.

grants pardon as God. *Who can forgive
sins,* asked the Jews, *but God alone?*
"But that you may know that the Son of
man hath power on earth to forgive sins,
I say to thee, arise." * And addressing
Mary Magdalene He pardons her all
the sins she has committed against God,
as though they were a debt contracted
with Himself, and because of the love
which she has for Him. Finally, He
judges as God : He announces that He
shall appear at the end of the world, in
the clouds of Heaven, surrounded with
power, and great glory, and that as a
sovereign He will pronounce the final
sentence on the assembled nations.

To crown all—after having assumed
all the titles and powers of God, He
claims also Divine homage. Faith :
"You believe in God, believe also in
Me." † Prayer : "Whatsoever you
shall ask the Father in my name, that
will I do, that the Father may be glorified in the Son." ‡ Love : He claims to
be loved above all ; to be loved more
than father and mother, more than
wife and children, to be loved with a

* Luke v. 20, 24. † John xiv. ‡ John xiv. 13.

love that does not flinch before death itself. To those who die for Him, He will give eternal life.*

How can we be unmoved when we think of the noble heart whence issued such words : of the great and sublime intellect which pronounced them—of the pure, spotless, light-giving conscience, out of which they sprung. Could He, the wisest, best, and holiest of men, be the most corrupt of men ? Could He, the humblest and most modest, be the proudest of men ? Could He, the ideal man, the typical man, He who possessed every human perfection, be after all the most infirm ? For such in truth would He be, if being only man, He identified Himself in His will, in His essence, and in his attributes with the infinite God, and that in a sense so wide, so deep, so unique that no man could make a similar claim for a moment without blasphemy and madness. Words such as these, moreover, which would be revolting to us if spoken by any other, and which in fact no other has ever dared to utter, appear quite

* Matt. x. 39.

natural to us from the lips of Jesus. They
appear to Himself yet more natural.
They are so nobly sustained by His Life
and works, that even those who do not
believe in Him dare not accuse Him of
fraud, or vanity, or ambition. Such an
accusation would contradict the common sense of mankind.

If, after all these proofs, yet another
proof were wanted of the consciousness
He possessed of His Divinity, I would
ask for no other than His method of
carrying out His great work. He has
but one way of enlightening and healing mankind, which is—to propose Himself to the world as an object of faith—
that is to say, an object for its love, admiration, and adoration. This in itself
we may observe, if not manifestly ab-
surd, supposes the consciousness of so
great a superiority, that we are obliged
to admit in Him who so speaks a presumption at least in favor of His claim
to the adoration of the human race. To
cure mankind, to heal its wounds, to
raise it to holiness, to endow it with
every virtue, Jesus Christ knows but
one way—Himself. Himself alone,

7

Himself, loved, known, adored. When He teaches, it is not to expound a system, but to reveal His own mind. When He suffers and dies, it is to manifest His love. And when on the cross He says that "all is finished," it is because He has unfolded His whole Soul, and thenceforth nothing more remains for Him to do. He leaves disciples behind, but do not think that it is to propagate His ideas. They are to preach Him Himself : to make Him known to the world, that He may enlighten all with His light. They were to serve, according to His own expression, as witnesses to Him in all parts of the world. This is the one mission that He gives to His disciples, and this alone is the mission which after eighteen centuries His Church continues to fulfil.

Attempts have often been made to draw a parallel between Christ and those great geniuses who, like Him, have collected and formed disciples ; and the name of Socrates suggests itself to all, because he also had the honor of dying for the truth. The resemblance, however, is but apparent ; the difference is deep and radical. Socrates preached the truth, Jesus Christ preached Himself ; Socrates considered all adhesion to his teaching that proceeded from confidence in himself, and admiration for his genius, illogical and unreasonable. Christ desired that the conviction of His disciples should rest on an entire faith in His word. Socrates, fearing to be an obstacle to truth, ever sought to blot out self, and carefully conceal his superiority, thus meriting an eternal remembrance. Christ, on the contrary, calmly and constantly affirms His own absolute superiority and the necessity of believing in Him. If Christ were not much above Socrates, He would be much below Him. The fact is, one taught as man, the other taught as God. And in making use of Rousseau's celebrated phrase, I would say—if the teaching of Socrates, and his method of conducting souls to truth, prove the philosopher, the teaching and method of Jesus Christ prove the God.

CHAPTER VI.

Jesus Christ claimed and received the worship
and the love of mankind.

WE will go still deeper. We have
seen that Christ was not satisfied with
calling Himself God, but He claimed all
the rights of God, and the homage due
to God. Now there is one act of homage which He demanded with peculiar
persistence, which He obtained in a
perfect degree, and in which He is dis-
tinguished from all others. I speak of
the love which Jesus Christ exacted
from men : a love so entire, so great, so
absolute, and so heroic, that the idea
alone of asking for such a love implies
the consciousness of the most divine
superiority, and removes our wonder
that, having dared to ask so much, He
should have been able to obtain it. And
as though human ideas were to be reversed in all that concerns this wonder-

ful Being, at the same time that He asked for love He foretold how He should be hated, and hated with a hatred as sublime as the love He would inspire. And what He foretold has been accomplished. At once loved and hated, adored and scoffed at, loved with a passionate love which eighteen centuries have not satiated, hated with a ferocity of hatred which eighteen centuries have not explained. My Jesus, I am going in search of Thy Divinity in the best way I can. I had a glimpse of it at first, sweet, and as though half concealed beneath the dazzling beauty of Thy Human Physiognomy. Now I seem to see its rays. The clouds have dispersed. The sky is clear. The sun, the sun of Thy Divinity shines forth. Help us yet a little that we may not arm ourselves against Thee with the last resource that remains to us—that of wilfully closing our eyes, and saying to the Sun itself—I see you not.

We have related in the course of this history the principal occasions when Christ put forward this peculiar claim to be loved, this design of winning and ruling all hearts.   Now I remark in this claim three things, which, when united, constitute a phenomenon, unique in the history of the feelings of man.

The first is that Jesus Christ wished to be loved *by all*.   Alas ! we find it difficult to gain the love of a few : how could we dream of winning the love of all ? Besides, who ever did dream of it ? No one : not even the founders of religious systems —the sense of helpless misery was too overwhelming. Besides, in order to be happy, do we find it necessary to be loved by all ?   In childhood, we wake into life under the eye of a father, and a mother, surrounded by little brothers and sisters who play and sing with us. This for a long while satisfies the cravings of our heart. Later, when we have grown up, we look amid the companions of our youth for some souls which sympathize with ours, and if we find one, we esteem ourselves happy.   And, later again, when that more passionate and more serious time of life comes, in which these first charms no longer suffice, what do we say to ourselves ? Some day I shall have a home, a pure and peaceful fire-side, some few friends, and if God allows me to meet with a noble, elevated, faithful affection, I ask no more for my happiness. And when we actually possess this, storms may come, the heavy weight of human affairs may oppress us, but we are not cast down ; for we have a shelter, a harbor, and a support. Such is the heart of man. He must have floods of light, floods of glory, floods of happiness. But if he find one drop of love it is enough for him. When, then, we see Jesus Christ so different, and hear Him declare that He desires to be loved *by all*, we are lost in amazement.

Yet this is not all. Not only does Jesus Christ require *all* to love Him, but He desires that each individual should love Him *above all*. He exacts the strongest, the most generous love : a love which tears men away from their pleasures : a love which, under certain circumstances, does not shrink from the testimony of blood. He asks of man a love, in presence of which every other love fades away.

In childhood you love your father and

your mother. They are objects of veneration to you. I know not why I
should say in childhood, for is there an
age in which father and mother are not
the objects of our veneration? It even
seems in proportion as we advance in
life, as years gather round their venerable heads, and we feel they are left to
us but for a brief space, our affection
increases, and rises to a kind of worship.
You have your father and your mother,
and you love them with all the affection
of your soul. Jesus Christ claims to
be loved more than your father, more
than your mother. "*He who loveth
father or mother more than Me, is not
worthy of me.*"

Or, say you are a mother, and in
your arms lies that little child which
you so ardently longed for, and which
you love so passionately. Jesus Christ
claims to be more loved even than that
child ; and to Him if necessary you
must even sacrifice that child. "*He
who loveth son or daughter more than
Me is not worthy of me.*"

And even in those still more intimate
affections, where two souls form only

one, Jesus Christ claims the right to
penetrate into their inmost recesses,
and demands to be still better loved.
" *He who loveth his wife more than
Me, is not worthy of me.*"

Can Jesus Christ ask such love ? Is
it not madness to ask it ? If He persist,
He must stand alone, abandoned by all,
the butt of the ridicule and contempt of
men. To obtain such love, even from
a few, would shock our sense of right.
Higher than father, mother, wife or
children, man knows only God. To
yield affection stronger than family
affection would be sacrilegious.

Jesus Christ goes still further in His
triumph over all the common feelings
of mankind. Not only does He claim
to be loved *by all;* not only does He
claim to be loved *above all;* but He declares that He will win to Himself this
mighty, wondrous, impossible love after
His death ! He was not loved during
His life, and He makes sure of being
loved after His death. Whilst He was
in this world, and bore on His countenance that charm which we were trying
to portray, He did not succeed in mak-

ing Himself loved. For were there any who sacrificed themselves for Him? Who accompanied Him in His last journey? Alone He mounted the hill of Calvary, and there, as the Scripture says, He sought one to console Him and He found none. And having been abandoned in His lifetime, denied in His lifetime, betrayed in His lifetime, not having been loved in His lifetime, to dream, that after He had disappeared, He should be loved with this mighty, heroic, unparalleled love :— once again this would be the dream of a madman, if it were not the thought of a God.

Yes! but perhaps He did not understand the human heart? Did He not know that intercourse is the great sustainer of love? did He not know how easily men forget? For a while, I allow, the tears of some faithful friend follow us beyond the tomb, but soon they who mourn, lie down in their turn in the same dust ; and the day comes when the indifferent passer-by treads under foot alike those who loved, and those who have been loved. So short

a time does love endure! And, not
having been loved during life, to dream
of being loved after death, to the end
of time! Can His clear, powerful,
robust mind cherish the anticipation?

Nevertheless, however strange may
be the anticipation, it has been surpassed by the result. Scarcely was He
dead before love awoke upon His tomb.
His cross was covered with kisses. A
whole generation of men and women and
maidens appeared, filled with passionate
enthusiastic love for Jesus Christ, who
took Him down, so to speak, from His
gibbet, and exclaimed while they covered His feet with kisses—Who shall
separate us from the love that we have
for Him? Shall hunger, or thirst, or
persecution? No, nothing can tear
from our hearts the charity of Jesus
Christ!

In vain have years gone by, and ages
succeeded one another. Time, which
destroys all other affections, has witnessed the growth of this affection.
Even Revolutions have been powerless
against it. In truth, Europe has passed
through many divisions, through fear-

ful convulsions ; it has been shattered into a thousand fragments—but there is one unity that has never been taken from it—the unity of the love of Jesus Christ. Photius could wrest the Greek empire from the crook of the Roman pontiff ; but he could not make Jesus Christ descend from the throne that He occupied in the heart of the Oriental population. Henry VIII. could throw the great English nation into schism, but the shadow of Jesus Christ, known, loved, served, and adored, still rests upon her. Luther was able to separate Germany from Catholic unity, but Germany still loves Jesus Christ. Finally, through whatever trials we have passed ourselves, after Voltaire and Rousseau, on the morrow of the Regency and the Revolution, does not Jesus Christ still shine forth in the adoration of the whole of France ? "Jesus Christ," M. Renan himself confesses, "is a thousand-fold more loved now, than He was during His life."

But a doubt arises in my mind. Has Jesus Christ been indeed loved as much as He desired ? Has He been loved

with that all-conquering love which in-
cites the soul to every sacrifice, with
that incomparable love which makes
every other love grow dim ?

If you doubt it, go and knock at the
door of one of those convents of Car-
mel where the mere enclosure provokes
you to fear or anger. Ask the young
maiden why, in the days of her youth
and her hopes, she abandoned all, to
hide herself behind an impenetrable
grating, and under a coarse woolen
garment. She will reply, *I love Christ.*
This is the love of Jesus Christ—a love
so strong that it created the Christian
Virgin, the Sister of Charity, the little
Sister of the Poor. It created the
apostle. It created the martyr. It
took man in his weakness, and selfish-
ness, and crowning him with the triple
diadem of virginity, of martyrdom, and
of the apostolate, it raised him to the
most divine pinnacles of love.

It has done yet more. For to suffer
and to die is not the perfection of love,
because it is not perfect sacrifice. The
perfection of sacrifice is, to see those
one loves, die. The loftiest height of

love in a mother, for instance, is not to give her own life for Christ ; it is to give Him the life of her child. And the world has witnessed this. There have been mothers who have so loved Jesus as to sacrifice their children to Him. He dared to ask it, and He obtained it.

Hardly had He died, before the Christian mother could say to her child, "I would rather see you dead, than see you betray Jesus Christ." And as she spoke, so she acted. She accompanied her child into the presence of his judges ; she descended with him into the Coliseum ; she mounted the scaffold ; she inspired him with her own enthusiasm ; and if she feared he were wavering, she threw herself on her knees, saying—"My child, remember that I carried thee in my bosom, that I nourished thee with my milk ; through pity for thy mother do not betray Jesus Christ !" No human language can say what a woman, what a mother must suffer at such a moment, what a Felicita, a Symphorosa, and so many others who imitated them, have suffered. We can only feel that an eternity of happiness with their children in their arms would not be too great a recompense for such sacrifices.

Who, then, is He who could obtain such a love? Who is He that once said to Himself in a little village of Palestine—I will be loved by all, I will be loved above all,—and who, having said it, obtained such a degree of love that all love grows dim before the love given to Him? Once more, What is He? And who shall dare to say that He was but man?

This is the great argument which struck the captive of St. Helena in those years of grace which God gave him to contemplate the things of eternity, after having played so stirring a part in this world. He said— " Jesus Christ claimed the love of man : He claimed that which is most difficult to obtain : that which a good man asks in vain from a few friends : a father from his children, a wife from her husband, a brother from his brother,— the heart : that is what He demanded for Himself. . . . He demanded it, and

He succeeded in obtaining it. From this fact I infer His Divinity."

He added : "Christ spoke, and thenceforth generations belonged to Him by ties closer and more intimate than those of blood : by a union more sacred and more imperious than any other union. He kindles the flame of a love which extinguishes the love of self, which prevails over every other love. . . . I have often thought of it, and it is what I most admire, and *what proves to me beyond a doubt the Divinity of Jesus Christ.*"

And insisting on the characteristic which I pointed out just now, that Christ desired to make Himself beloved after His death, he said : "I filled the multitudes with enthusiasm, and they were ready to die for me, but my presence was necessary, the electric effect of my glance, my voice, a word from me. Now that I am at St. Helena, now that I am alone and nailed to this rock, where are the courtiers of my misfortune ? Who troubles himself about me in Europe ? Where are my friends ?" And going back from himself to Louis XIV., and looking at the great king with a glance unbiassed by the vanity of human things, he added, —"The great king was hardly dead but he was abandoned in the solitude of his bedroom at Versailles, neglected by his courtiers, and perhaps the object of their derision. He was no longer their master : they saw only a corpse, a coffin, a grave, and the horror of approaching corruption. Yet a little while, and such will be my fate : this is what will happen to me. What an abyss between the depth of my misery and the kingdom of Jesus Christ, preached, loved, adored, and living throughout the whole universe ! . . ."

And Pascal before him, jotting down these flashes of genius on scraps of paper which were afterwards collected as relics, wrote these three sentences, which from his pen would have made such a wonderful chapter : " Jesus Christ desired to be loved : He was loved : He is God ! "

8

He is loved, & He will be loved forever; He is God !

CHAPTER VII.

A wonderful counterproof.—Jesus Christ prophesied that He would be persecuted with an
  unquenchable hatred.—He was thus persecuted, and He is still thus persecuted.

HOWEVER striking, nevertheless, this
proof may be, we do not realize its full
force except in connecting with the
second prophecy of Jesus Christ, a
prophecy not less wonderful than the
first, and not less wonderfully realized.
Christ did not only ask for love and
obtain it : He prophesied that He should
be hated, and He has been hated, and He
is hated still. Here is the counterproof, and I own that it is a thing
which baffles me still more. To me it
is quite incomprehensible that a lowly,
gentle, meek mechanic should publicly
say : "To the end of the world I shall
be hated :"—that He should gather
round Him twelve other mechanics,

meek and gentle like Himself :—that
He should say to them, "You also shall
be hated unto death "—that He should
preach a lofty, pure, and noble doctrine,
and that He should say to them, "Till
the end of the world this doctrine will
provoke furious outcries : "—that dying
at last in such suffering as ought to
have touched all hearts, He should declare that His cross would be also an
object of hatred :—that there should
be men who could not look at it without outbursts of anger :—this I repeat is
incomprehensible. For if it is difficult
to make oneself beloved, is it then so
easy to make oneself hated ? In one
of his admirable discourses on Jesus
Christ, Père Lacordaire said, "Who
amongst great men has been loved ?
Who in war ? Who in wisdom ? Tell
me one who has left love upon his
tomb." I would borrow his words and
say, Who has been hated ? What
king ? What philosopher ? Tell me of
one man, a great man, a philosopher, a
founder of religion, who after death
has excited hatred. If the memory of
some for a time has been pursued by

116 *The Divinity of Jesus Christ.*

public indignation, time passed on,
forgetfulness succeeded, and hatred disappeared. Only Jesus Christ has been
honored with an inextinguishable hatred.

If, then, it appears to me strange that
Christ should have prophesied for Himself this hatred, I find it yet more
strange that this prophecy should have
been realized. For what is there to
hate in Jesus Christ? Is it His character? But clearly, there never was one
more beautiful on this earth. Is it His
doctrine, His Gospel? But you confess
that no book can be compared with it.
What then is it that you hate in Jesus
Christ?

You will say—It is very simple.
What I hate is falsehood, and falsehood
deserves to be hated in proportion as it
meets with greater success. For eighteen centuries this imposture has dazzled the world, and this is what I hate.

If you are certain that Christ is an
impostor, then I understand your feeling ; but we may defy any sane man to
entertain such a conviction, and this
for a thousand reasons, and for one in

particular :—which is, that there are found too many educated and sincere men who have believed in His Divinity. Bossuet, Pascal, Leibnitz, Grotius, Newton, great men for eighteen centuries have studied, and, nevertheless, have bowed down before Jesus Christ : they have believed in His Divinity, and have made considerable sacrifices during their life for this belief. For there is this difference between those who do not believe in Jesus Christ and those who do believe : the latter make sacrifices for their convictions, the former do not.

But be it so : let us suppose that Jesus Christ is an impostor. In that case the love which we feel for Him is false, the hatred you have vowed against Him is true. That consequently which ought to be fruitful, that which ought to renovate the world, that which ought to transform man and society, is the hatred of Jesus Christ : for if love which is deceived in attaching itself to this Chimera, to this idol, does such great things, what will not the hatred which upsets it accomplish ? Well !

What has this hatred of Jesus Christ done for man ? Where are its works ? What nations has it rescued from vice and barbarism ? What souls has it consoled ? Where are its Sisters of Charity ? its Brothers of Christian Doctrine ? Where are its little Sisters of the Poor ? There are men in want of bread : you who hate Jesus Christ —do you beg for them ? There are men who die in pain. Do you nurse them ? Oh you who hate Jesus Christ ! I look for you beside the sufferer and the mourner, and I do not find you.

You have done nothing for man :— what have you done for God ? You have torn the love of Jesus from a heart : have you filled it with greater love of God ? There are still, even now, whole nations prostrate at the feet of idols. You who hate Jesus Christ—where are your apostles ? I do not ask where are your virgins ? and still less do I ask, where are your martyrs ?

Once more : What is it that has engendered this hatred of Jesus Christ ? Mahomet was not hated, nor Numa, nor Zoroaster. No other founder of religion has met with hatred. Nero, Tiberius, Domitian—monsters such as these were hated only for a time. Hatred could take no root; it withered on their tomb. Jesus Christ alone has been honored with an inextinguishable hatred. Whence does this proceed?

It proceeds from this—that we only hate what is a restraint and an obstacle to us: anything that oppresses and crushes us. When Nero was weighing down the world with all the weight of his infamy, I can understand that he was hated, and I am not surprised that Tacitus should have had but one regret, —that of not having a pen severe enough to brand him with eternal infamy. But now that Nero has long passed away, and his vices sleep despised and impotent with his bones, who hates Nero? who hates Tiberius? who hates Domitian? Hatred indeed would be too much honor for such as they; they only deserve contempt.

And I do not wonder that a St. John, a St. Polycarp, a St. Ignatius should manifest towards all the great sophists of the first ages—Ebion and Cerinthus,

Arius and Nestorius—indignation and anger. They were powerful in their day: they * divided Christ : they injured the Church : they stopped the way of Christianity. But now that they have been overcome in this great conflict ; now that only their lifeless dust remains, and their errors are incapable of seducing even a child, are you astonished that hatred has ceased ?

Are not our sentiments modified even as regards Voltaire himself ? In my youth I knew a venerable old man who had lived before the Revolution, and had seen Voltaire in all his triumph reigning, dominant, crushing Jesus Christ with his sardonic laugh : he could not speak of Voltaire without something of that anger which rings through the works of the Comte de Maistre. We have seen all that Voltaire would have laid waste, bloom again ; we have seen that revive in greater splendor which he thought to destroy : we now look upon Voltaire as vanquished. We know that his works which were so much read by our fathers will not be read by our children ;

* I. Corinthians, i. 13,

and in proportion as his influence wanes, our indignation and anger subside. Such is the human heart! We hate all that is an obstacle to us : we hate everything that tramples on us. But when the foot that trampled on us is turned into dust, how can we hate it any longer ? Hatred ceases, and gives place to contempt.

Jesus Christ is the only man towards whom hatred has never relented ; the only man whom contempt has never reached. What is the meaning of this, except that He never lays down His arms, that His influence never wanes, that He is always a restraint to the passions, that He is always king, and always conqueror ?

But this is not all. There is in hatred something much deeper. It sometimes separates souls which God had destined to live together in an intimate union, and then it assumes fearful proportions. Hatred between two brothers, born of the same mother, nourished with the same milk, whose branches should have intertwined during their whole life, and mutually sheltered each other, is something dreadful, and is seldom, if ever, extinguished. Even worse is the hatred between man and wife. And when there is this hatred, just where there should be most love, note this peculiarity. I can understand that a soul, having surrendered itself entirely to true affection, and having met with betrayal and desertion, should hate its betrayer. Well might that soul say with the poet—

Je vous ai trop aimé pour ne pas vous haïr.

But it is not so. It is not the victim who hates, but he who has been faithless, he who has violated all his promises. And the purer and more beautiful is the victim, the more intense is the hatred. Were she less faultless, she would be less hated, because her superiority would be less felt. And if to beauty and blamelessness she had added benefits ; if her hands were full of blessings, which she had showered on her thankless foe ; if she still continued to shower down on him these blessings—then, immeasurably superior to him in her purity and in her love, she would call forth in that treacherous soul a passion which nothing could satisfy !

That which we see on earth happens sometimes between man and God. When man has been loaded with favors, and his soul has not been great enough to respond by gratitude for what God has done for him, it happens that love, becoming bitter, turns into hatred, and that God becomes the object of an undying hatred.

Such was the passion kindled in the Emperor who left a name so mournfully renowned—Julian the Apostate. From the temple where he had been brought up, from the blessings of God which had been showered down on him, from the loving protection of the Church which had preserved his crown ; not having a heart large enough to respond, he turned against the Church, and hatred was enkindled in his soul. He was not content with destroying the Church, he wished to bury her in infamy. All the power of the Roman Empire was employed for this purpose, and his hatred, increasing as he advanced in years, knew no intermission till the day when, on the fields of Persia, he died exclaiming, " *Thou hast conquered, O Galilean !* "

Our immortal poet, Racine, in his *chef-d'œuvre*, " Athalie," has represented the same passion. What is that treacherous character who appears from time to time, and serves to throw into relief the greatness and the nobleness of the other characters ? Whence does He come ? Who has excited this hatred in his heart ? The high-priest tells us at the commencement in a celebrated verse :—

> Ce temple l'importune, et son impiété
> Voudrait anéantir le Dieu qu'il a quitté.

Such is hatred of God ! Such is hatred of Jesus Christ ! For they are never separated. He who loves God, loves Jesus Christ. He who hates Jesus Christ, hates God. To human eyes they make but one in love and hatred. To have acquired such a solidarity, must not Jesus Christ be God ?

CHAPTER VIII.

These facts cannot be denied.—They cannot be
explained if Jesus Christ be only man.

IT would seem that when brought
into contact with facts such as these,
and with claims, not only extraordinary
in themselves, but still more extraordinary in their realization ; in having
to deal, moreover, with the words in
which Jesus Christ so clearly, distinctly,
and consistently affirmed His Divinity,
and exacted for it the homage of all—
two courses alone are left to those who
will not believe ; either to attack the
testimony of Christ Himself, if they
hold the Gospels to be true ; or to throw
doubt on the Gospels themselves.

To attack the testimony of Christ, is
to suppose either that through lack
of intelligence He could, in good faith,
be mistaken about His own nature,
or, that through lack of sincerity He
intended to deceive us ! In either case

Jesus Christ sinks to the lowest level. There is no longer any consistency in His life, nor any intelligible explanation of His character. Everything in His life and character falls to pieces, and becomes contradictory ; and the mind recoils from the numberless impossibilities which arise. "Can there be any union between light and darkness ? " said the prophet. Evidently not. Sunshine and darkness, truth and falsehood, absolute purity and deceit, sublime intelligence and gross delusion, cannot be found together in the same soul. They are conflicting elements. If light is there, it must chase away darkness. If Christ is what we have seen Him to be, so pure and so holy, so completely humble and modest, so perfectly calm and gentle in His light, free from all exaggeration and enthusiasm, He could not be mistaken as to His real nature : He could not have believed Himself to be God. He could not have said He was God if He did not believe it to be true. This, the bright side of His character, drives away the other absolutely and entirely, as the sun drives away darkness. Do we not feel there could be no place for such a fundamental and astounding illusion, and for the intoxication of such a dream about His Nature in a mind like His, clear as the sky ; in a heart such as we have seen His to be, absolutely pure, and transparent as crystal ; in a character healthy and vigorous in every respect, always strong, and always master of itself ; and still less could there be room for the artifices and miserable contrivances which would have been necessary to persuade the world to believe in it. This is evident, with evidence clear as the sunlight.

If, on the contrary, you believe that Jesus was mistaken, that through lack of intelligence He believed Himself to be God, or that through lack of sincerity He wished to make us believe it— be it so ! But then He ceases to be holy : He ceases to be great. You must blot out the saying of Pascal, "He was humble, patient, thrice holy in the sight of God, terrible to demons, and sinless." You must say He was nothing of the kind ; He was just the

contrary. How could He be humble
and modest, and intelligent, if He believed Himself to be God when He was
only man? How could He be holy if,
knowing that He was not God, He
could nevertheless say that He was?
How could He be great if, in order to
make men believe this, He employed
miserable and unworthy means? And
yet, was not Christ great? Was He
not gentle, modest, humble, divinely
beautiful in life and in death? Was
not His every breath, and the faintest beating of His heart, pure with
a perfect, ideal purity? Then what are
we to believe, what are we to say?
Where else is there anything certain—
anything that I can admire, and love,
and venerate? Where is the True,
where is the Good, where is the Beautiful, if Jesus Christ be but illusion,
falsehood, fraud, moral deformity,
united, by some monstrous mystery, to
greatness the most divine that has ever
been seen? Weigh that well. A character must be consistent. It cannot inspire at once contempt and love, adoration and disgust. There is no middle

path. Such as Jesus Christ presents Himself to the world He must necessarily either fall into dust, or we must fall at His feet. He is all, or He is nothing.

Perhaps you think you can lessen the difficulty by transferring the accusation from Christ to His Apostles and Evangelists? You may say it was they who invented this fable, and who persuaded us of it? But you will encounter a host of impossibilities. "You must find," says Bossuet, "an apparent cause for the most unshaken faith ever exhibited in the world, yielded by men most timid and incredulous, in truths far beyond our comprehension, under the severest trials. Deception does not go to such length, nor last so long, and madness is not so consistent. For to follow to a conclusion the reasoning of the unbelievers, what do they think of our holy Apostles? That they had invented a fine fable, which they were pleased to announce to the world? Would they not have made it more probable? That they were foolish and imbecile, and did not know what they

9

meant themselves ? But their life, their writings, their laws, the holy discipline which they established, and finally, the event itself, proves the contrary. That artifice should invent so clumsily, or folly carry out so happily, is unheard of. The project does not betoken men of cunning, nor its success men destitute of sense. They tell us, ' We have seen, we have heard, we have touched with our hands this Jesus, risen from the dead ; and not once only, or for a minute, or in private, but often, for a lengthened period, and before many witnesses.' If they speak the truth, what reply remains ? If they are inventing, what do they aim at ? What advantage, what reward, what recompense for all their labors ? If they expected anything, it was either in this life, or after their death. To hope for anything in this life ? The hatred, the power, the number of their enemies, and their own weakness, would not allow of such a hope. Thus they must look to future ages ; and either they must expect from God happiness for their souls, or they expect from men glory and immortality for their names. If they expect the happiness which the true God promises, it is clear that they do not aim at deceiving the world, and if the world imagines that the desire of making a name for themselves in history could reach these uneducated minds even in their fisher's boat, I can only say : If such as Peter, and Andrew, and John, in the midst of so much opprobrium and persecution, could foresee from afar the glory of Christianity, and the honor which we pay them, I require no stronger proof in order to convince all reasonable minds that these were divine men, enabled through the Spirit of God, and the ever invincible power of truth, to see in the extremity of oppression the secure and certain victory of the good cause." *

Such are some of the difficulties, stated with the logic, the vigor of mind, and the eloquence of Bossuet. But there are others, and one in particular absolutely insoluble, which Rousseau himself had caught a glimpse of, and which modern criticism has carried to

* Bossuet, "Panégyrique de S. André."

a degree of evidence which admits of no reply. You say that the Apostles invented this character of Christ—His life, His death, His scheme, His character : Rousseau gives the answer. "The inventor would be more wonderful than the hero." Modern criticism goes farther, and says : "The inventor is an impossibility. To invent the character of Jesus, a second Jesus would be needed."

I have already cited, in treating of the Gospels, very remarkable observations of Channing, Goethe, and the anonymous author of *Ecce Homo,* showing how impossible it would have been for the Apostles to create a character which was so completely above them. For, let me insist on this : it was not a question, as was said formerly, of inventing a fact—the fact of the Resurrection for example—a thing in itself impossible, nor of embellishing and arranging certain events. It was necessary to create a character which should be consistent with these facts and events. Now, if the Apostles had tried, they would have created a human character, and very probably a Jewish character : a perfect Rabbi like Hillel or Gamaliel, at the most a prophet like Elias or John the Baptist ; and if, endeavoring to surpass any known type, they had exaggerated the true proportions, they would not have made a real character. For they were utterly incapable of creating a character such as the one we have seen unfolded under our eyes—that is to say, a character, the most novel, the most original, utterly beyond all the ideas of the time, opposed to all the aspirations of the Jews, the least human, or rather the most superhuman—at once human and divine, and nevertheless real. They call Him man : where then could they have found the idea of this perfect sanctity, this spotless life, this complete freedom from fault, never before found in man. They believed Him to be God : why then did they represent Him as so weak ? Did they not know how to describe a courageous death ? "Yes," says Pascal, "for the same St. Luke represents the death of St. Stephen as more full of strength than that of Jesus

Christ." * And if Jesus Christ never uttered the ineffable Sermon on the Mountain, the discourse at the Last Supper, the prophecies of the ruin of Jerusalem and the world, and those vivid descriptions of the future, who could have invented them ? " Suppose," said Parker, " that Plato and Newton never lived—that their story is a lie :— but who did their works, and thought their thought ? It takes a Newton to forge a Newton. What man could have fabricated a Jesus ? None but a Jesus." †

It is then impossible that a single man should have conceived and in-vented in all its aspects a character like that of Jesus, which so completely sur-passes all the experience of the human mind. The difficulty is greatly in-creased by the fact that, instead of being created by one alone, He must of ne-cessity have been created by several. And it avails nothing to say that each Evangelist presents to us a different

* Pascal, " Pensées. "
† Theodore Parker, " Discourse of Matters per-taining to Religion," p. 271. Chapman, 1846.

Christ. This is false to begin with—as we have proved. Moreover, on this hypothesis, instead of one miracle you have four to deal with. The Jesus of each Evangelist, in fact, is wonderful, inimitable, absolutely superior to the writer who described Him. Besides, He is complete in each Gospel. Take but the Jesus of St. Matthew. Destroy the three other Gospels—you would doubtless lose some treasures. But the Jesus of St. Matthew will suffice to call forth the adoration of the world. Take all four Gospels, and blend them in one. The manner, the style, the language, and the point of view of each writer is unlike that of the others, but the Christ of whom he writes is always the same —a distinct exalted individuality, never to be confused with any other. In the pages of four different authors Christ appears the same, divinely beautiful in each, and in all raised so above His humble painters that far from being able to create Him they were even unable to copy Him. This avowal escapes from M. Renan, in one of those moments when the truth forces itself even on those who deny it. "So far from Jesus having been created by His disciples," he says, "He appears superior to His disciples in everything. The disciples, with the exception of St. Paul and St. John, were men without invention or genius. Upon the whole, the character of Jesus, *far from having been embellished by His biographers, has lost in their hands.*" *

If they were incapable of embellishing it, if they could not do it justice, if "it entirely surpassed the mind of His disciples," as Parker says ; "if it surpassed even," according to Channing, "the human intellect"—they could not have created it. It existed independently of them, before them, and is greater than they are. It is then in every sense real, in every sense historical, and this is the final verdict of modern criticism.

What shall we say now, in completing this subject, of an hypothesis which had a certain vogue in Germany, but never in France, in spite of many efforts to introduce it ? for if French

* Renan, " Vie de Jésus."

genius has its weaknesses, it glories in a clearness which would not allow of its being employed in such mists. I speak of the mythical hypothesis of Strauss. Neither one writer nor many acting in concert or not, could have created a character which so completely and absolutely surpasses the experience of the human mind—and it is asserted that it came from the slow, hidden, unconscious incubation of a people. The most beautiful book that has ever enlightened, consoled, and enchanted mankind is the creation of everybody, that is to say, of nobody. That face and form which not even the master hand of a Raphael, a Fra Angelico, a Leonardo, or a Van Dyck could worthily portray, whose beauty no art, however beautiful, can represent, was made of itself! It came forth by successive touches from the heart and the feelings of the first Christian communities! But let me here ask one question. Who made these communities? How did they become Christian? Was it not the Christ, the Christ known, loved and adored as God and man, who made the

Christian people? Then, how could these same people have made the Christ? You will not accept the historical date of the Gospels? Good! but you cannot deny the date of the Acts of the Apostles, nor the authenticity of the Epistles of St. Paul. Now these two monuments are full of Christ. He appears there as the center, the bond, the cement, and the architect of all the first Christian communities. How could it be they who created the Christ, since it is from Him that they sprung. If it were they who by successive and unconscious strokes made this sublime portrait which has enchanted the world, by what were they themselves enchanted?

But, however, this question is no longer discussed. It has gone by. It has succumbed, not beneath the efforts of reason, because what is illogical and irrational has such a charm for certain minds! Two facts have finally disposed of it: the discovery of the Syriac version of the Gospels by Dr. Cureton, and the discovery of the Codex Sinaiticus by M. Tischendorf. Time, and a great deal of time, would be required

for such an incubation : here no such
time elapsed. This is what these two
archæological discoveries have proved.
This discovery consigns Strauss's book
to the waste-paper basket.

CHAPTER IX.

The new life, and the transformation of the world, cannot be explained if we reject the Divinity of Jesus Christ.—Jesus Christ regenerated the world by stamping His likeness upon it.

BUT let us lay the Gospels aside also —the Gospels in which the dazzling beauty of the Son of Man lives, and will ever live, without ornaments, without grand phrases, in the simplest style —a beauty which will suffice to defend it against all doubt, and attract every soul to itself sooner or later. After all we have other means of forming a judgment on the character of Jesus Christ. We may measure it by its shadow, as Parker says, or rather by the light which it has cast on the world. We can appreciate Him by the wonderful effects of His word, by the results of His life and death. What was the world before He came? What has it become since? Let us try to measure

the change He has caused in it : the
intellectual, moral, and religious beauty
which He has communicated to it—we
shall find at the same time a new measure, and a very just one, of the greatness of Jesus Christ.

Strange phenomenon ! Jesus made
the world in His own image and likeness, and it is by this that He has regenerated and transformed it. Those
grand characteristics of His mind and
heart, His loftiness of thought, His
tenderness and purity of feeling, His
breadth of comprehension as displayed
to us in the Gospels, are reflected in the
modern world, and it is this which dis-
tinguishes it from, and makes it superior to, the ancient world. The ancient world was plunged in idolatry, in
ignorance of God, in superstition so
deep and inveterate, that Plato, with
all his genius, felt himself incapable of
dissipating it, and called loudly for in-
tervention from above. And now this
God, whom Jesus called His Father, is
ours. This pure and spiritual worship,
this adoration in spirit and in truth,
this beautiful religion founded on purity

of heart, on the divine paternity, and the brotherhood of man, is the religion of all, even the most lowly. Like Jesus, we know and feel ourselves to be Sons of God. God is not outside us, and far off; He is within us, He dwells in our hearts, and makes our life godlike. The dullest existence, the one most forgotten by men, has yet an insight into a corner of heaven. And who shall say to what perfection the virtues that shone in the heart of Jesus—His humility, obedience, zeal for the glory of God, love of men—have attained in certain souls? Nowhere, doubtless, has the Divine Model been equaled, but discouragement has never arisen from the inability of reproducing it in its perfection. And, as nature multiplies its efforts, varies its shades and colors, brings forth millions of species of roses in order to realize the type, so each of the virtues of Christ has created during eighteen centuries thousands of men who have made the sublimest efforts to try and reproduce something of His inimitable beauty. The world has been filled with the perfume of these efforts, and has owed to them, besides the general character of religious aspirations, a supernatural fruitfulness, of which the ancient world had not even the idea.

And this is not the only feature of His character that Jesus Christ has imprinted on modern society. Jesus, who in heaven saw only His father, on earth saw only souls. For Him there was neither great nor small, neither rich nor poor, and I will say with the Apostle, neither male nor female, neither young nor old. Wealth and rank, greatness and poverty, old age and youth, and all other outward distinctions were but transparent veils, through which His most pure eye perceived alone that majestic presence which is called a soul. Now this character of high spirituality is the second character of the modern world. Towards the close of ancient history men had regard only to the exterior, and esteemed none but the rich and powerful. They crushed the weak, women and children, and trampled the poor under foot. Suddenly a strange thing occurs. The soul imperceptibly takes possession of the first place. And as a consequence, woman, despite her weakness, is raised : the child is raised, even the sickly child whom the State condemned to death : the slave is raised while keeping the chains he will soon lay aside : the poor man is raised, and will see his rags touched with respect by the rich. It is an unheard-of, unhoped-for, irresistible revolution. The great and the strong pass to the second place. There is infinite consideration bestowed on the lowly, and a new society is built up on gentleness for the little one, on respect for woman, on love for the poor, and on the self-respect of all in a holy equality.

And as one of the features of the beauty of the Son of Man is the universality of His love, as one cannot think of Him without seeing Him fastened to the cross, His arms extended to embrace the world, the barriers between nations fall : the love of country, without ceasing to have a share in the heart of man, becomes less exclusive ; beacons are lighted all along those sea-coasts where formerly profit was made from ship-wrecks ; the word *hostis* has no longer

any meaning ; the human race is born—
that is to say, the great republic of
brothers, separated still by interests and
language, but having at least three
bonds which make them one, notwith-
standing the barriers of mountains and
seas—the bond of blood, the bond of faith
and the bond of love.

And this is but the commencement.
Here is the most divine and royal feature which the beauty of Christ imprints
on modern society. Modern society,
like Him, has something infinite, incom-
mensurable, never to be satisfied, which
constitutes its pride and its beauty ; and
here is the origin of its progressiveness.
Look at the ancient world. Everything
in its way is perfect. Each man attains
his ideal, and realizes the good and the
beautiful as far as his nature appre-
hends it. In the modern world, on the
contrary, the aim is never reached. All
aim at a beauty—shall I call it imagi-
nary, since no one attains to it, and since
all lament that it is beyond their reach ?
Listen to the ancient world. In art, in
philosophy, in poetry, what an expression of satisfaction ! It found and real-

10

ized the beautiful, and was happy. How different from this long aspiration, this incessant lamentation of the modern world : "Ah ! if I could arrive at absolute beauty ! If I could find eternal truth ! If I could make the good, the beautiful, the noble, the holy live in me ! "

The old world erected its temples, set up its statues, composed its dramas and its glorious epics, all with a certain finish. The new world, in its art, in its philosophy, in its poetry has nothing which it considers as finished. It has not the courage to finish anything : its ideal so far surpasses any reality. The Parthenon expresses the desire of beauty satisfied ; the Cathedral of Cologne the soaring aspiration of love unsatisfied.

I can never think without amazement of the strange conception of the gods in Homer. They are crowned and recompensed in the Elysian fields, but they are not happy—they are full of regrets. And what do they regret ? The earth they have quitted, this life, the light they had here below. Great as they are, they estimate themselves as shades only. Light, beauty, life for them is in this world. Darkness is above where they are. Listen to them ; listen to Achilles. Does he desire a greater splendor? No, he regrets his strength, his former valor. And all are the same. Unfortunate shades, who live turned towards this earth which they have left, and whose only consolation is to come back and wander among the living. We, on the contrary, remain unsatisfied though we live in this new world of Jesus Christ amidst all the splendors of creation and art. We dream of a beauty greater than any beauty we have ever known, which we despair of realizing here below. Even when we find ourselves in heaven we shall scarcely be satisfied. We shall go from light to light, always seeking something yet more beautiful, retaining our desires, our aspirations, but not our grief ; for desires as they arise will be ever satisfied. Such is the human mind in the modern world. It has been completely changed.

This grand phenomenon of history, on

which I do not further insist, evidently presupposes an extraordinary event which corresponds to it, and effected the transformation. There must have been a moment when the ancient world came to an end, and the new commenced. Some influence must have been exerted over souls to drive them in the new direction. When was this moment? What was the first step in this endless progress? Who opened this era? There is but one reply—Jesus Christ. It is absolutely certain that the ancient world comes to an end at the Cross of the Saviour, neither sooner nor later, and that the new world begins then. The cross is the stopping-point of the fall, the point whence renovation begins; and if Jesus Christ is God, all is to be understood and explained. But if Jesus Christ is not God; if He has substituted idolatry for idolatry; if He deceived mankind, and if by this falsehood, or by this illusion, He has regenerated the world, then everything is to me wholly unintelligible. All my ideas of certainty, of truth, of justice, of virtue, and, I will add, of cause and effect, become

confused to my mind, and even the idea
of God is enveloped with a veil.   What
Napoleon said is true :—" In short, and
this is my last argument, there is no God
in heaven, if a man could conceive and
execute with full success the gigantic
design of appropriating to Himself
supreme worship, and usurping the
name of God."   And I add, if he could,
while usurping the name of God, and
plunging the world into idolatry, at the
same time regenerate it.

CHAPTER X.

History is inexplicable, and faith impossible unless we believe in the Divinity of Jesus Christ.

YES, and this is my conclusion. If Jesus Christ be God, everything is consistent, and all the parts hang together —His life, His doctrine, His miracles, the wonderful effects of His appearance on the earth, and even the very time and place in which He did appear. When the fulness of time was come, when the faith of the infancy of the world had become feeble, and when from every lip was heard the question, Who shall show us any good ?—when human hearts had become disgusted with the burden of sin—then God sent His Son into the world to bring help to man, who was sinking beneath his burden. He appeared in the central point of history, in the capital of the world, full of grace and truth, free from error and from sin, innocent and

holy, practising every virtue, overflow-
ing with the tenderest love for God,
with the most divine pity for man, and
He sealed a most pure life by a sublime
death. Outwardly He is man, but the
light of His divinity manifests itself
through the ideal beauty of His Humanity—very gently at first, then with
greater vividness, at last bright and
dazzling like lightning. He appears
quite impregnated with divine life, and
men, in uniting themselves with Him,
find in His mind, in His heart, in His
strength, in His entire life, an expan-
sion of their own. What more simple,
what more consistent, what worthier of
God, what more honorable to man !

Let us suppose nevertheless that
Jesus Christ be not God : that the hero
of this drama be but an innocent dupe,
or a clever impostor—what do you
gain ? Do you escape the mystery ?
On the contrary, instead of one mystery
there are ten or a thousand : a chaos
of inexplicable difficulties, of contradictions whence there is no issue.

Yes ! if Jesus Christ be not God, if
He be but a man, a crucified Jew, it is

inexplicable that men should have believed in Him, believed in Him during His life, believed in Him after His death : that they should have believed Him to be the Son of God, His only Son, born of a Virgin, risen from the dead, and ascended into Heaven in the presence of five hundred disciples. That is inexplicable. Can you, being man, and the child of man, call yourself God, and bind yourself to act as God ? You could not keep up the character for a quarter of an hour. You would be seen through before the end of your first discourse. And nevertheless men believed Christ to be God :— and His enemies, who were watching Him closely, could not find a single vulnerable point, and could not find at any moment that the man appeared and betrayed Himself. This is inexplicable.

And what is still more inexplicable is that men should have believed in Him with such intensity of faith, with such ardor, purity, and heroic generosity. And not a few men only. I might almost say the whole world has believed in Him with a belief amounting to passion, madness, and readiness to sacrifice everything—even life.

Count up, if you can, the millions of martyrs who, during eighteen centuries, in every land and in every phase of civilization, have hastened to death as to a feast, set on fire by their invincible faith in the divinity of Jesus Christ. Count up the hermits who have left all for Him, whose life was a prodigy of abnegation, patience, and sacrifice. Count up the virgins who, renouncing the noblest joys of earth, took Him for their spouse, and consecrated to Him their pure virginal thoughts. Count up the many holy wives, devoted mothers, and innocent maidens who owed to Him the beauty of their souls. Count up the mourners, innumerable also, who in the midst of their tears have welcomed sorrow in consoled and resigned hearts. Count up those again who, beginning their life anew for Him, have firmly and resolutely climbed the rugged heights of penance.

For what is wholly inexplicable, if Jesus Christ be not God, is, not only that men have believed in Him—believed in Him so far as to lay down their lives for their belief, but also that they should have been regenerated through this belief. What is wholly inexplicable is that this falsehood or this dream, whichever you call it, should have overthrown paganism, destroyed the religion of the senses, and purified the poisoned air of the ancient world. What is wholly inexplicable is that it should have produced the greatest characters, and the most heroic virtues : a St. Agnes, a St. Cecilia, a St. Augustine, a Charlemagne, a St. Louis,—that it should have brought forth Christian Europe, that it should have created the Church : that at the end of eighteen centuries it should still be able to calm passions, and inspire heroic actions, to stop the tears of mourners, and assuage sorrows which seem beyond consolation, and that it should strip death of its most appalling terrors. What is inexplicable is that a falsehood should produce such effects, and that it alone should produce them. A great orator once exclaimed—Ah ! if I wished to gain a worthy idea of truth, I would go and kneel at the foot of the cross. I would say to myself—it is but a dream, an error, a conscious or unconscious falsehood,—and seeing the tears it has dried, the sorrows it has consoled, the misfortunes it has softened, remembering the heroic virtues and self-sacrificing devotedness it has inspired, I would say to myself—O my God! if error can do such things, what then will not truth accomplish when its reign shall come?

But how can I dare to invoke the name of truth? What is truth? Where is truth? Where is truth in history? If you do not believe in Christ, in whom do you believe? Do you believe in Cæsar, in Alexander, in Socrates? "But the facts about Socrates, which no one doubts, are less strongly attested than those relating to Jesus Christ." Where is truth in religion? You say Christianity is but a falsehood. Much more so then is Paganism, Mahometanism, or Buddhism. Nothing remains in the religious archives of the human race but error

succeeding error, and the most divine
of human aspirations has been a snare.

Natural religion remains, you will
tell me : but do you find in natural religion a single dogma, a single precept
which rests on deeper and more solid
foundations than the divinity of Jesus
Christ? God must be adored and
prayed to, you say. And why? Because the conscience of man demands it,
because the voice of humanity teaches
it. But for eighteen centuries the
voice of humanity has proclaimed the
duty of adoring Jesus Christ, and conscience declares that this adoration is
reasonable. Once more, then, where is
truth? Where is it in philosophy, in
morals, in jurisprudence, in political
economy? You believe in property, in
the legitimate transmission of the fruit
of your labor, and you are right in believing in it. But this fact of property,
the basis of the social world, does not
rest on truer, more numerous, more
certain, and more irrefragable proofs
than the Divinity of Jesus Christ. If
this is not proved, you can prove nothing ; and the hand which dethrones

Jesus Christ, willingly or unwillingly, must also dethrone God. For God after all, from the height of His throne, has seen the triumph of falsehood and wickedness. He has seen a simple mortal arrogate to Himself the Divine Nature. He has seen the world dazzled, fascinated, falling at the feet of their false god, and He has permitted it. He has permitted that the world, instead of being corrupted by this idolatry and adoration of falsehood, should be thereby regenerated. He has permitted the purest flowers to spring from this corrupted soil and He has not intervened. He has seen the human race incapable of distinguishing between truth and error, since if truth is anywhere it is barren ; whilst Christianity, which is error, falsehood, and idolatry, is fruitful and rich in blessings—the sublime source of goodness and beauty. God has seen all this, and has held out no helping hand to poor deluded men, His children !

O my God, my God ! into what abysses do we not fall, into what inextricable chaos does not the human mind precipitate itself, when it refuses the light Thou hast prepared for it. And what anguish does it not prepare for itself if it loves the truth, and feels unable to live without it. Wandering in darkness, coming into collision with a thousand insoluble problems, such an one is not long in becoming acquainted with the most painful of temptations—he will close his eyes and will not even try to see. The spirit of darkness watches by the pillow where his sleep is broken and his suffering soul disturbed, and in the hours of sleeplessness a voice makes itself heard—"Dismiss these questions, abandon thy search of truth, shut thine eyes, try to forget and to sleep." Oh Jesus, have pity on these suffering souls, on these poor and noble searchers after truth. They have not fled from light, they have not desired darkness, and had they done so, Thine is the heart, oh Jesus, to conquer them by excess of love. Let but one ray of light, however feeble, dart from Thy wounded feet and hands and from Thy open heart. Let them see Thee, oh Jesus! and they will be saved. For

Thou Thyself art the most convincing proof that the Religion Thou hast founded is true, and the dullest mind will be enlightened, the faintest heart will be healed, if only Jesus Christ appear.

THE END.

SACRED HEART RETREAT
NEWBURG ROAD
LOUISVILLE, KY.